Supporting Communication Disorders

Supporting Communication Disorders

A Handbook for Teachers and Teaching Assistants

GILL THOMPSON

David Fulton Publishers

London

David Fulton Publishers Ltd
The Chiswick Centre, 414 Chiswick High Road, London W4 5TF
www.fultonpublishers.co.uk

David Fulton Publishers is a division of Granada Learning Limited,
part of the Granada Media group.

First published 2003
10 9 8 7 6 5 4 3 2 1

British Library Cataloguing in Publication Data
A catalogue record for this book is available from the British Library.

ISBN 1 84312 030 5

Typeset by Keyset Composition, Colchester, Essex
Printed and bound in Great Britain by Thanet Press Limited, Margate, Kent

Contents

About the author

Gill Thompson has a BA in speech therapy and is also a qualified teacher. She has an MEd in special education and has experience as a speech and language therapist in England, France, the USA and South Africa. She has lectured at University College Worcester, delivering a module on communication disorders, and currently works as a special educational needs teacher and SENCO (special educational needs coordinator) in primary education.

Acknowledgements

I am grateful to my colleagues for their support, advice and contributions to this book. A special thank you to my husband, Colin, for his encouragement and patience. Thanks also to the parents and children who have provided me with the experience for writing this book.

I would also like to thank Jude Bowen at David Fulton for her guidance in compiling my first book.

Introduction

An increasing number of children enter school with poor communication. Children will come from a variety of different backgrounds and their experiences will have shaped their development of speech and language in the first few years of their lives. Some of them will have very little speech when they start school and their ability to listen and process verbal information may be limited. However, after a few weeks of school, with opportunity to adjust to the routine and structure of a new environment, it is hoped that the child will learn to respond and participate, to interact with other children and adults and be part of a class. Speech and language development is usually helped by the wealth of multisensory experiences, teacher encouragement and peer contact. Many of the children for whom teachers have initial concerns, will no longer be such a concern by the end of their first term at school.

How do we, as teachers, recognise those children who have a more profound and significant difficulty and what do we do about it? How do we go about getting professional help and advice and what intervention can be planned into the daily routine of school?

Throughout my work as a speech and language therapist, I tried to develop close links with schools but was aware that the system was not always ideal and teachers often felt that they needed more support in addressing the needs of children with poor communication skills.

Since returning to college and training as a teacher, I have realised that the development of speech and language and the basis of speech disorders is not necessarily part of the teacher's basic toolkit and, although fundamental to children's learning, this is an area that has long been omitted from initial teacher training.

I was asked to plan and deliver a module for teachers and teaching assistants on the subject of the management of children with speech and language disorders. This book is the result of that course and the feedback I received regarding what was useful and of value in mainstream classrooms. It is not intended to be a textbook on speech and language, but more a practical handbook offering information, ideas and guidelines to teachers in their planning and intervention for those children who are presenting with communication difficulties. Many of the suggestions could be incorporated into programmes to be delivered by teaching assistants or parents.

With the focus on inclusion, teachers are expected to deal with a vast range of disability among the children they teach and to have the knowledge and skills to address each child's individual needs appropriately. As classroom teachers, we spend vast amounts of time planning the curriculum and assessing and recording children's progress and attainment. We are able to recognise when a child is struggling to achieve the skills we are teaching but need to understand the underlying causes and the nature of the difficulties before we can tackle the problems and put effective strategies in place.

Aims

This book aims to:

- provide a general understanding of the underlying causes of speech and language difficulties;
- provide a workable framework for nursery teachers, class teachers and special educational needs coordinators (SENCOs) in primary education to help with initial analysis and assessment of speech and language difficulties;
- offer guidelines for referral, strategies for effective management within the classroom and ideas for activities and resources to help individuals or small groups of children;
- provide suggestions for planning programmes of intervention which can be delivered by teaching assistants or class teachers;
- facilitate cooperative work and sharing of information between teacher and therapist;
- bridge the gap between theory and practice, providing a range of information and practical advice.

1 Communication difficulties

Identifying the specific nature of a communication problem

Speech and language is one of the most difficult areas of the curriculum to assess. This is because it depends very much on the situation, the individual child, their background and experience. It is often hard to know what you should be looking for and how far from 'normal' the child's speech is.

Verbal communication involves two main components:

Speech, the mechanical aspect of communication, is the physical ability to produce the sounds, words and phrases. *Articulation* is the term used for the motor process of speech production. It is the accurate and precise movement and coordination of the organs of articulation (e.g. tongue, jaw, teeth, lips) to produce sounds. *Phonology* is the organisation of those speech sounds to form words and phrases.

Language is the understanding of concepts and the way sound patterns, words and phrases relate to one another to carry meaning and information. The acquisition of *vocabulary* and *grammatical structure* are part of the process of language development.

There are many influences on the child's developing *expressive* (output) and *receptive* (understanding) skills. These may enhance or suppress the development of speech and language, depending on the quality of the child's sensory and physical functions. The development of communication relies on the child's ability to take in sensory information, to process that information and to become competent at using the organs and muscles that are necessary to produce speech. It is also dependent on the range of stimulation provided and the experiences offered in the formative years prior to school entry. The developing child may experience difficulties in one or more areas of communication and even a short-term problem, such as an ear infection, may influence the way that a child perceives certain sounds as they are learning them.

A preschool child may have inaccurate articulation or 'babyish' language structure and other developmental milestones may have been delayed (e.g. crawling, sitting, walking . . .). At school entry, some of these immaturities may persist.

1

In many cases, children with poor communication skills at preschool or school entry will rapidly show improvements when placed in the structured environment of a nursery or reception class. The influences of their peer group, the need to communicate and the wealth of everyday language activities all provide motivation and stimulation for the development of speech and language.

In some cases, however, the difficulties may persist. There could be specific reasons for the delay in developing speech and language skills and these will need to be monitored and investigated (see Chapter 8 – Specific speech and language disorders).

Action

If the child does not make the expected progress within the first few weeks, or if there appears to be a more severe difficulty which is making it hard for the child to participate fully in the class activities and/or social or play situations, then the child's speech should be investigated further.

1. Discuss your concerns with the parent (they may be equally concerned or may not have noticed a problem, but their input is vital and a legal requirement).

2. Check whether the child's hearing has been tested.

3. Check if there has been any previous involvement with a speech and language therapist (this information is not always passed on by parents at school entry).

4. Discuss your concerns with other involved members of staff, including the special educational needs coordinator (SENCO) and the head teacher.

5. Following observation, the SENCO may decide to place the child at **School Action** level of the special educational needs (SEN) register and draw up an Individual Education Plan (IEP). This will indicate areas needing specific observation, strategies for helping the child and details of any in-class support or differentiation that may be required.

Once a problem has been identified, the teacher needs to initiate a process of observation and evaluation of the child's communication skills so that a clearer picture of the specific areas of difficulty, progress or deterioration, environmental influences etc. can be monitored and assessed.

The SENCO, the class teacher or teaching assistant, can carry out observation. Results of observation should be used to inform the planning of a programme of support or intervention.

As a general approach, I would suggest:

- set aside specific times for observation;
- draw up a rota or list of children to be observed;
- choose a selection of activities for observation (interaction with another child, play house activities, structured play activities, sharing a book, participation during circle time or literacy hour class/group activity);

- observation sheets or a diary should be at hand for use during selected times and also for any impromptu moments when it might be important to jot down a relevant comment.

The whole range of activities that take place in the nursery/school classroom, playground or any other part of the school can provide opportunities for informal assessment and observation. Children need to be observed in a range of situations, in different social groupings (pairs, friendship groups, activity groups etc.) and curriculum areas (sharing books, sand and water play, areas set up for observation, e.g. fish tank, pets, display corner, science investigations, working out a practical number problem etc.). You may also find it valuable to observe the child interacting with a parent, brothers or sisters, as speech may be more spontaneous and relaxed in a familiar situation. This could be set up at school or could involve a home visit.

Communication is one of the areas where it is easy to make a 'wrong' or unfair assessment. Be aware that a shy child may take time to feel comfortable with a group of other children or with unfamiliar adults, that a child may revert to 'baby' talk when feeling insecure and that some children find it difficult to respond to direct questioning in an unfamiliar situation.

You may choose to use the observation chart and articulation record provided (Figure 1.1), or use one of your own devising. I would suggest that you include the following areas to give a thorough and broad investigation:

General abilities

- Group participation
- Social interaction with peers
- Listening and responding to stories
- Describing and relating real and imaginary events
- Giving and responding to instructions
- Asking and answering questions
- Communication with family members

Specific abilities

- Articulation/phonology (details of wrongly articulated sounds, whether initial, medial, final, vowel/consonant, consistent or random substitutions etc.) – see Chapter 3
- Difficulty repeating/learning new sounds or words
- Imitation of tongue movements
- Use of vocabulary
- Sentence formation (specify any immature or incorrect structures)
- Ability to communicate needs
- Reluctance to communicate
- Use of any alternative means of communication, i.e. pointing, gesture, signing, taking an adult to show them etc.

Observation Chart

Child's name:

Observed by:

Observed behaviour	Date	Date	Date	Date
Listening to a story within a group				
Responding to group questions				
Responding to questions directed at him/her				
Interacting with another child – play				
Communicating with a familiar adult				

Comments:

Figure 1.1 Observation chart. © Gill Thompson (2003) *Supporting Communication Disorders*, David Fulton Publishers.

When a profile of the child's communication abilities has been achieved, it will be necessary to establish whether this is a problem that can be dealt with in school, with the support of the parents or whether it is going to necessitate a referral to a speech and language therapist.

If the child has significant communication difficulties which are preventing full participation in class activities and improvement has not been apparent *in spite* of support and encouragement in the classroom, then it will be advisable to seek a professional opinion.

Guidance for referral to speech and language therapy

Action

Once a referral is made and an outside professional becomes involved, the child needs to be placed at **School Action Plus** of the SEN register. This indicates that advice has been sought from an outside agency and that the therapist is contributing to the IEP.

The following are of note regarding the referral process.

- The parents will need to be informed and their cooperation should be sought (this is not always forthcoming but if it is, it can make all the difference).
- I have found that the best way to make a referral is to ask the child's parents/carers to speak to their general practitioner (GP) and request that the child has a hearing test and is seen by the speech and language therapist. It is also possible for the school or parents to refer directly. Whichever referral route you choose, it is helpful to send information regarding your concerns and the nature of the support already provided at school. Copies of any assessments you have done and a brief summary of the child's difficulties give a clearer picture to the therapist in the initial stages of referral.
- There are usually waiting lists, so be prepared to provide a programme of support at school while you wait for the child to be seen (see suggestions for general activities – Chapter 4).
- When the child is given an appointment, contact the speech and language therapist and introduce yourself (letter or phone) and explain that you would like advice on how to work with the child at school and some suggestions for support. Parental permission will need to be given before the speech and language therapist can disclose this type of information. It is a good idea to start this link early so that the therapist can get permission from the parents when they take the child to the initial visit.
- Offer to send the therapist details of your own observations and support work so that it is clear what has been done already.
- Suggest a home/clinic/school book so that any weekly work can be supported at school and incorporated into the IEP/weekly planning.

The child is likely to be seen for a block of approximately six weeks and then given a break. Make sure that you have information for making your own programme of work at school once the therapy period is completed. A decision should be made as to whether the class teacher or the SENCO will liaise directly with the therapist and be the school contact. This avoids any misunderstandings and creates a good channel for communication.

Speech and language therapy is generally the responsibility of the NHS (National Health Service) and children with identified needs will be seen by the speech and language service provided by the local NHS Trust.

In the *SEN Toolkit* (DfES 2001a) the following recommendations are made:

> Wherever possible, therapy for children attending school should be carried out collaboratively within the school context. In some cases, children may need regular and continuing help from a speech therapist, either individually or in a group. In other cases, it may be appropriate for staff at the child's school to deliver a regular and discrete programme of intervention under the guidance and supervision of a speech and language therapist.
>
> (DfES 2001a: Section 12, p. 17)

Action

Where a child has ongoing communication difficulties that do not respond to intervention at this level and are having a major impact on the child's learning and social skills, the school may decide to present evidence to the LEA in support of a request for Statutory Assessment.

---

2 The development of speech and language

How do speech and language develop?

As adults with well-developed abilities to communicate and express ourselves, we do not necessarily realise how complex the developmental process of speech really is. We take for granted the ease with which we speak. It is, however, important to understand the developmental sequence of speech and language acquisition so that you can pinpoint where the child is and where they should go to next.

Stop for a moment and say your name slowly, focusing on the movements that your tongue and lips make, the way your jaw opens just the right amount for each sound, the way you automatically control the flow of air from your lungs and the vibrations in your voice box. We do this without being consciously aware of how we speak. Say the following phrase in different ways, using varying inflection to express a statement, a question and a rebuke – *'You are running.' 'You are running?' 'You ARE running!'* Once again, we are able to do this without a great deal of thought or effort. How did we learn to do this? How can we set about helping a child master these skills if they have not managed to learn them on their own?

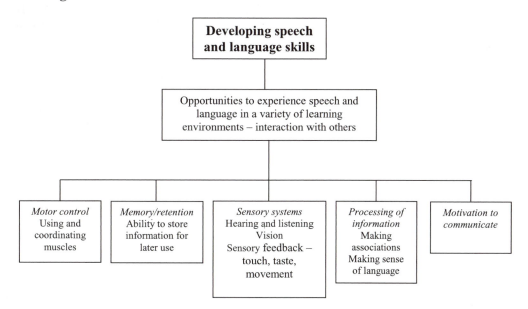

Figure 2.1 Developing speech and language skills

By understanding the basics of normal speech and language development (Figure 2.1) and the mechanics of sound production, you will be more able to unravel the child's problems and begin to rebuild their speech skills.

The sequence of development

The newborn baby begins life by vocalising as air is expelled from the lungs and through the larynx. In the first few days of its life, the child becomes conditioned to the association between vocalising and comfort – it cries aloud and is either fed or rocked in its mother's arms. This begins the progressive cycle of sound and response as communication develops and is refined to become increasingly under the child's control. Different sounds are experimented with during the babbling phase when a child practises and enjoys making strings of repetitive sounds, experiencing the sensory feedback as each sound is vocalised.

By entering into a two-way interaction with other persons, the elements of both sound production and cognition become bound together as the child develops both physically and neurologically. The young baby soon realises that by making sounds, facial expressions, movements, it can influence its environment. As the child matures, it becomes more able to use expressive skills to effect – gesture, actions and language.

In the early years, speech and language are used to communicate and to explore and learn about the child's immediate environment. Later these two functions become more specialised and sophisticated and follow parallel paths in the progression of the child's general development.

Early language development is closely linked with the development of other skills – motor, cognitive, social. The child's abilities to focus attention, to learn through play and to form social interactions are central to the development of language. The different components making up the language of communication are each important in their own right, yet inextricably intertwined to create the complex system by which we exchange information, express our feelings and intentions and share so much of our lives.

In order to comprehend the developmental process, it is useful to be aware of the initial stages of speech and language, which set out the pattern of normal development (Figure 2.2). It can only serve as a guideline, as every child progresses at a different pace, but can demonstrate the basis of the acquisition of communication skills thus providing a starting point for understanding how and why some children are slow to develop these skills and the extent to which their development may be delayed. It also demonstrates the extent to which other developmental areas such as motor skills and cognition influence the progress of speech and language development.

Speech and language – developmental sequence

(Based on development profiles by A. Gesell, J. Lindon and C. Hood in Gesell 1966)

0–3 months

First sound is a loud cry. Subsequent sounds are linked to physiological activities such as breathing and feeding – yawn, sneeze, belch and cough.

8–20 weeks

Makes vowel sounds and has an auditory awareness of sounds.

3–6 months

Spontaneous vocalisation – consonants and vowels, some syllables as well as gurgles, coo and chuckles. More responsive to the human voice and may turn his/her head on hearing a familiar sound.

Interaction with an adult brings about the changes to widen the child's outlook. This experience is a prerequisite for the comprehension of words. The mouth is used to explore objects using tongue and lips to provide sensory feedback.

10 months

Now eating increasingly solid food and by exercising the muscles needed for chewing, is also laying down neuro-motor patterns for speech. By increasing the dexterity and coordination of lips, tongue, chewing and swallowing mechanisms, the child is developing control over the muscles used for articulating speech sounds. May have a vocabulary of one or two 'words' and will respond to his/her own name. Starts to wave 'bye-bye' and to respond to own reflection in a mirror.

1 year

Responds to some verbal commands such as 'give it to me' and attracts attention using several 'words', which have a definite meaning. Understanding is developing at a faster rate than expressive ability.

18–21 months

Begins to use words and gestures. Uses 'inflected jargon', which imitates sentences but has little meaning to the listener. Responds to simple commands and may refuse to do these by saying 'no'. Starts to use 'bye-bye', 'all-gone' and other familiar early phrases. Repeats single words that are said to him/her and asks for the toilet, food or drink.

2–3 years

Asks questions 'What's that?' Talks in simple terms about immediate experiences and repeats much of what is said to him/her. Refers to self by using a pronoun – 'me go out', 'me want drink' and vocalises readily. Not yet able to properly engage in a two-way conversation.

4–5 years

Increasingly communicates through speech and carries on long involved conversations. Can tell a story, although this may be a mixture of real and imagined events. Is eager to find out how things work and what things mean and asks a lot of questions.

Personality and social behaviour will shape the child's speech and language use and the rate of development may be significantly influenced by the amount of speech and language that the child has been exposed to in their home life and preschool experiences such as playgroup or nursery.

Figure 2.2 Speech and language – developmental sequence

3 The sounds of speech

How are sounds made?

The young child spends a long time imitating and practising sounds, learning to coordinate the different parts of the oral musculature, vocal cords and breathing to allow sounds to be linked together to create words, phrases and ultimately, and gradually working towards, the use of continuous speech.

It helps to know which sounds are made by which organs of speech as you can then group sounds together when teaching them – working on those sounds made by the tongue or on sounds that are made at the front or back of the mouth etc. This will make it easier for you to help a child to progress from learning a single sound and then putting it into an initial word position.

The organs of articulation

The main organs of articulation (*articulators*) are the **tongue, lips, palate, jaw** and **teeth**. Figure 3.1 shows these and the other organs of articulation. The **larynx** is the organ responsible for producing a voiced sound as air is expelled from the lungs and passes through the vocal cords causing them to vibrate. The **articulators** shape the sound.

Vowel sounds are made with an open mouth and are created by the lips and the changing shape of the oral cavity caused by opening and closing the jaws.

Consonants are shaped by different organs of articulation working together, which affects the sound as it passes out through the mouth.

Consonants can be pushed through closed lips causing an **explosive** sound – /p/, /b/.

They may squeeze between two different articulators causing **friction** – /f/, /v/, /s/, /sh/, /ch/.

They may be made by one organ **tapping** on another – /t/, /d/, /n/, /l/, /k/.

They may be made with complete **closure** of the lips so that the sound is pushed out through the nasal cavity – /m/.

The organs of articulation

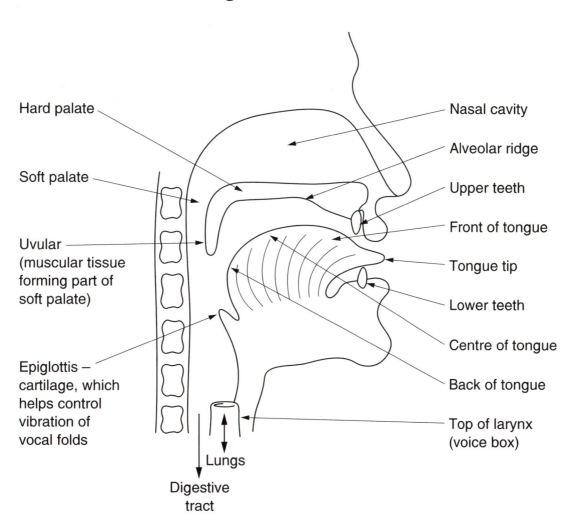

Figure 3.1 The organs of articulation

They may be made at the **front** of the mouth – /**m**/, /**p**/, /**b**/, /**s**/, /**t**/, /**d**/, /**sh**/, /**ch**/, /**j**/ or at the **back** – /**k**/, /**g**/.

Some sounds are articulated in such a way that the articulation is seen by the listener – /**p**/, /**b**/, /**m**/, /**f**/, /**v**/, /**th**/ – while others are made less visibly and are difficult to observe.

Some sounds are produced without causing the vocal cords to vibrate. There are pairs of sounds which are articulated in the same way but one is '**voiced**' and the other is '**voiceless**', for example /**p**/ is voiceless whereas /**b**/ is voiced. Other pairs of sounds are s/z, t/d, k/g; this subtle difference in voicing is one that many children find difficult.

Sounds that are visually explicit are often easier for young children to learn than those that rely on auditory and kinaesthetic (sensory–motor) awareness. To develop the fine coordination for correct sound production, the child needs to be able to listen, watch and have good mobility of the speech organs. The location of sound production is as follows.

Location of sound production

Lips – p, b, m, w

Lips and teeth – f, v

Tongue and teeth – t, d, th

Tongue and palate – n, r, l, s, z, sh, ch, j

Back of the tongue and palate – g, k, ng, h

Figure 3.2 shows the lip, tongue and mouth positions for producing sounds and Figure 3.3 shows the lip shapes for vowel sounds. This background knowledge is also of value when doing an assessment of a child's speech, as it can show a problem with a particular area, for example /**th**/ or /**f**/ and /**v**/, where the sound is not being made correctly.

Lip, tongue and mouth positions for producing sounds

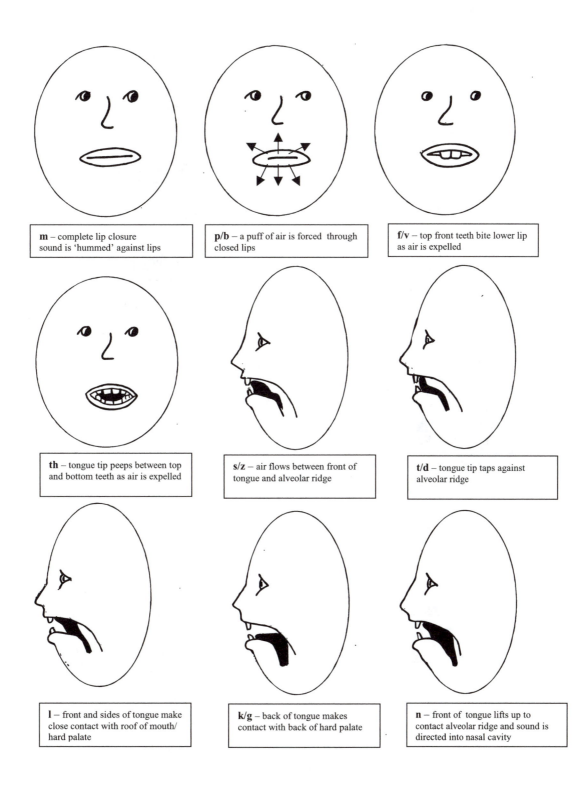

Figure 3.2 Lip and tongue positions for consonants

Lip shapes for vowel sounds

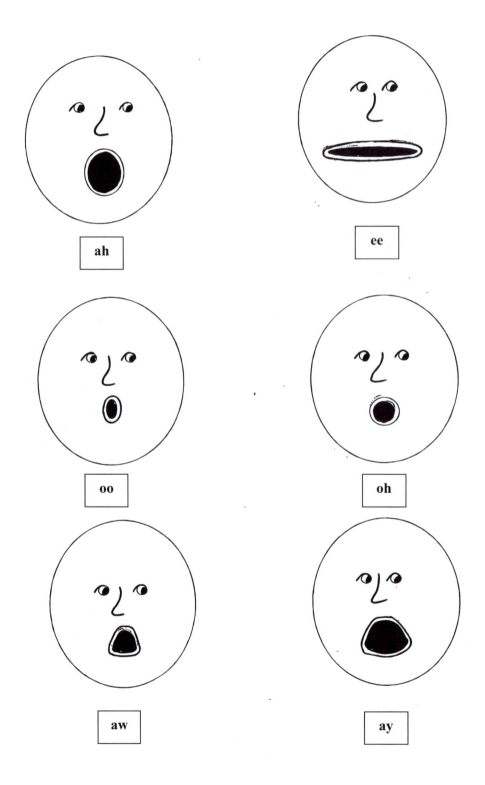

Figure 3.3 Lip shapes for vowel sounds

Teacher assessment of speech sounds

Assessment by the teacher and/or SENCO usually takes the form of observation within the classroom environment. The teacher is often aware that the child's speech is difficult to understand but finds it hard to pinpoint exactly where the child's difficulties lie. It is useful to have a simple way of listening to the child's speech and recording any errors.

There are a variety of standardised assessments used by clinicians but these are not easily available to teachers and require a detailed knowledge of phonetics. In order to provide a basic picture of whether the child is making a few isolated errors, is unable to produce a range of sounds or is failing to articulate sounds in a particular word position, the basic articulation screen described here (and recorded on the assessment sheet shown in Figure 3.4) is a quick way of recording the child's speech profile. It can be used to pass on information when making an initial referral or to plan an interim programme of support for a specific child.

I recommend using the pictures shown in Figure 3.5 on individual cards or in a flipbook. Present them to the child in a quiet one-to-one situation without distractions. The child should feel relaxed and comfortable with the situation and should be encouraged to name the picture spontaneously. If a prompt is needed, the child should attempt to imitate the word. This is worth noting on the record sheet. When making a record of how each word is articulated, it is advisable to tape-record the process, as you will find it easier to go back and complete the assessment when you can listen in greater depth to the recording. When you are more familiar with the test, you may wish to devise a simple formula of marking the sheet such as one dot for correct, two for an error so that the child is less aware of the idea of failing or making mistakes.

If you feel that a child is not able to access the pictures provided, you can use different images, photo cards or objects for some of the words. For an older child, you may prefer to use word cards for the child to read aloud.

Pictures/words for articulation assessment

pig, puppy/dog, cup/coffee, tap, ball, bus, rabbit, web, man, mummy, thumb, wheel, water, shower, cow, fish, knife, nose, van, oven, dive, ladder, bed, feather, bath, banana, sun, arrow, lolly, castle, zip, lizard, cushion, chair, matches, watch, jam, hedgehog, sledge, bucket, girl, burger, box, hat, behind, sock

The pictures in Figure 3.5 can be photocopied and you may wish to enlarge and colour them to make them more attractive and accessible to the child.

Assessment of Speech Sounds

Name: Age/ D.o.b.:   Date of assessment:

Sound	Initial		Medial		Final		Comments
p	pig		puppy		cup/tap		
b	ball/bus		rabbit		web		
m	man		mummy		thumb		
w	wheel/water		shower		cow		
f	fish		coffee		knife		
v	van		oven		dive		
t	tap		water		hat		
d	dog/dive		ladder		bed		
th	thumb		feather		bath		
n	knife/nose		banana		man/van/sun		
r	rabbit		arrow				
l	ladder		lolly		ball		
s	sun		castle		bus		
z	zip		lizard		nose		
sh	shower		cushion		fish		
ch	chair		matches		watch		
j	jam		hedgehog		sledge		
k/c	cup/cow		bucket		sock		
g	girl		burger		pig		
x					box		
h	hat		behind				

Figure 3.4 Assessment of speech sounds

Figure 3.5 Pictures for articulation assessment

© Gill Thompson (2003) *Supporting Communication Disorders*, David Fulton Publishers.

Figure 3.5 Pictures for articulation assessment (continued)

© Gill Thompson (2003) *Supporting Communication Disorders*, David Fulton Publishers.

Please note that selected speech sounds are based on the phonetic sound rather than the way the word is spelled, i.e. the /s/ in nose is pronounced /z/, /dge/ in sledge and hedgehog is pronounced /j/, /st/ in castle is pronounced /s/. Sounds are presented in their single form rather than being part of a consonant blend and the assessment looks at each sound as it appears in an initial word placement, medially and in a final position.

Word placement

e.g. *initial* consonant	/**s**/un	/**t**/ap	/**b**/ed
medial consonant	me/**ss**/y	wa/**t**/er	ra/**bb**/it
final consonant	bu/**s**/	ha/**t**/	we/**b**/

Children with communication difficulties will sometimes present with an isolated problem associated with the pronunciation of certain sounds. There may, however, be a cluster of difficulties including a range of articulatory errors, receptive and/or expressive language, word-finding difficulties, fluency difficulties etc.

The analysis of sound production is only one part of the overall assessment process and you will need to look at other aspects of the child's communication in order to see a more complete profile (see Chapter 6 – Language – assessment and ideas for intervention programmes and Chapter 8 – Specific speech and language disorders).

When you have completed your observations and have looked at the child's use and understanding of language, you may want to record your findings on the 'Speech and Language Checklist' provided (Figure 3.6).

The 'Sound Assessment' chart in Figure 3.7 will help you decide how to set about helping the child who has a specific disorder with the production of sounds. It is intended to guide you towards activities which can be incorporated into class planning, one-to-one support and intervention groups, based on the initial assessments that you have carried out.

See Chapter 4 (p. 30) 'Listening for the correct speech sound' to help complete the Sound Assessment Chart.

When you have analysed the child's speech and found that certain sounds are being made incorrectly, you will need to decide how to proceed. If the child is making a large number of errors and speech is unintelligible, it would be advisable to seek a professional speech and language assessment.

Speech and Language Checklist

Name: Age/D.o.b.:

Date of assessment: (✓ to indicate concern)

Is he/she difficult to understand?	
Speaks audibly (not too loud or too quiet)?	
Reluctant to communicate?	
Articulates initial consonants? ('cat')	
Articulates final consonants? ('cat')	
Articulates medial consonants? ('lorry', 'yellow')	
Uses initial consonant blends clearly? ('tree', 'blue', 'sky')	
Final consonant blends? ('sink', 'belt', 'tent')	
Does he/she omit sounds or syllables?	
Confuses certain sounds consistently when talking?	
Specify any deviant sounds:	
Able to distinguish between /t/, /k/, /s/, /sh/ in words spoken to him/her? (take/cake, told/cold, ship/chip, bat/back, light/like)	
Has difficulty repeating sounds?	
Has difficulty imitating tongue movements?	
Has difficulty learning new words?	
Relies on other forms of communication? (pointing, signs, gestures)	
Uses a poor/limited vocabulary?	
Uses immature sentence structure? Specify:	
Relies on what other children are doing to follow instructions?	
Follows simple verbal instructions?	
Follows 2–3 part instructions?	
Interacts verbally with other children?	
Listens and follows a group story?	
Responds appropriately to questions?	

Comments:

Figure 3.6 Speech and language checklist

© Gill Thompson (2003) *Supporting Communication Disorders*, David Fulton Publishers.

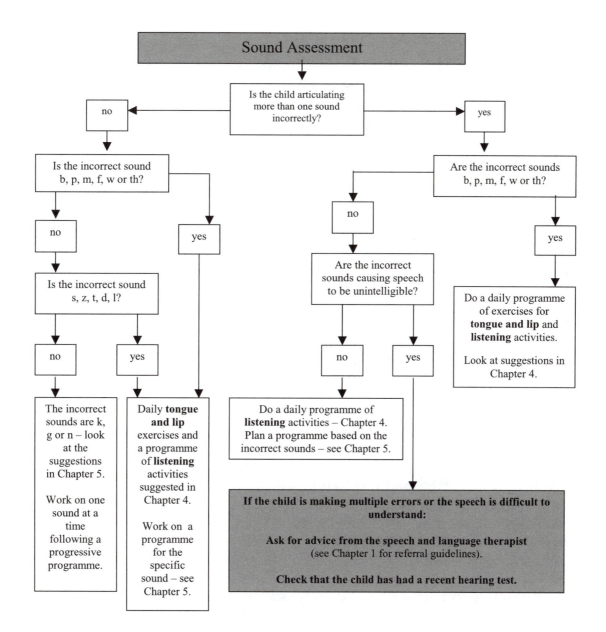

Figure 3.7   Sound assessment flow chart

What causes poor articulation?

If a child's speech is not within normal limits for his or her chronological age, there may either be a '**developmental delay**' or, if the development does not follow the normal developmental pattern, it may be the result of a specific '**disorder**'.

Developmental delay

If the child has a developmental delay, speech may be immature and sounds may be produced at a level expected of a much younger child – this is where the sequence of development is useful for planning. Delayed speech and language development can also be caused by a variety of factors which can include learning difficulties, lack of experience and stimulation, periods of illness or hospitalisation, or reaction to the birth of a sibling or a marital breakdown or similar significant emotional trauma.

Disorders that may affect the development of speech and language

Hearing

Articulation problems frequently stem from hearing difficulties. A child who has frequent colds and ear infections may have intermittent, fluctuating hearing difficulties that are not necessarily apparent. A deviant pattern of speech sounds may be established if the child's hearing is affected, even for a short while, during a crucial developmental stage. Check whether the child has had a hearing test recently. This can be done via the child's GP or the school nurse. Hearing difficulties can include the following.

- The child may be unable to discriminate between certain sounds, for example p/b may sound the same and even if he or she watches your face, they will look the same as well. The child will not necessarily notice the difference in 'voicing' between the two sounds.
- High frequency sounds may sound similar and be difficult for the child to discriminate – s/sh/ch/t/th.
- Sounds that are made inside the mouth – r/l/t/d/n/k/g – carry no visual cues to show how they are made and children may substitute alternative sounds in an attempt to imitate.
- The individual sounds in a word or phrase may not be heard distinctly.

Sensory–motor (kinaesthetic)

Some children have a poor sensory or kinaesthetic feedback and awareness. If this is related to the mouth and tongue they can find it difficult to control these organs of articulation or to be aware of what their lips and tongue are doing. Imagine trying to get your tongue round the sounds of a new foreign language immediately after a visit to the dentist! This type of difficulty may be due to **verbal dyspraxia**. A child with verbal dyspraxia will have difficulties making and coordinating the precise movements required in producing spoken language. The child may find it difficult to imitate sounds and tongue and lip movements, may produce inconsistent substitutions for sounds and have problems organising sounds into words, phrases and sentences. Verbal dyspraxia is a disorder of the child's motor programming system and can have a profound effect on the child's communication skills. It may be an aspect of a more general **dyspraxia** or **developmental coordination disorder** in which children display difficulties with both gross and fine motor coordination, organisational and sequencing skills.

In a child who has cerebral palsy or has experienced neurological trauma, there may be **dysarthria,** a disorder which affects the learning and development of motor skills for speech. These children may also have related difficulties with chewing and swallowing, breathing control and lip closure and may dribble as a result. Where any of these conditions is suspected, they will need to be professionally diagnosed.

Physical disability can also cause difficulties with the development of speech. Cleft lip and/or palate (congenital abnormalities of the mouth and face which can also be caused by adverse influences during pregnancy such as drugs or virus infections) are usually successfully repaired at an early age but there may be residual problems with lip closure and palate movement.

There are also specific syndromes that have associated speech and language difficulties, particularly those where poor muscle-tone and coordination are symptoms, such as Down's syndrome or Prader Willi syndrome.

If there are significant difficulties and the child is very hard to understand, you should seek advice from a professional. Referral may, however, take some time and a general programme of games and activities (see Chapter 4) to increase the child's awareness of sounds and overall motor control can be initiated. Even minor articulation or phonological difficulties can cause problems with reading acquisition, as the child may not hear the difference between individual sounds and may find the whole process of learning letter sounds and understanding the concept of 'beginning' sounds very confusing.

With the young child, it is always better to approach intervention through play and informal activities and to encourage success in an immediate way, for example using stickers on a chart or on the child, verbal praise, group acknowledgement of success. (For more information on specific speech and language disorders see Chapter 8.)

4 Making sounds – teaching sound production, sound awareness and basic listening skills

The following classroom activities can be used with children who speak unclearly, have difficulty producing sounds correctly or who are reluctant speakers. They are intended to help the child imitate sounds, lip and tongue movements and facial expressions, thus increasing awareness of the way that sound can be changed and played with. This type of activity is part of the normal 'babbling' but may well have not been practised enough by the child at the appropriate developmental stage. Some of the suggestions will encourage the child to listen carefully to sounds that they hear. The intention is to make these activities enjoyable and light-hearted and to encourage an enthusiasm for joining in.

These general activities can be used in a one-to-one situation or can be incorporated into group work. They would be good introductory work while you wait for a more detailed programme from the speech and language therapist and would be appropriate for children with delayed speech development, hearing difficulties or problems discriminating between sounds, verbal dyspraxia, physical abnormalities or congenital disorders affecting speech production.

Games and activities for tongue and lips

These activities can be used in a one-to-one situation or with a small group and are an enjoyable way of increasing the child's awareness of the speech mechanism and developing control over tongue, lips, palate and breathing. They can be used at the beginning of a more specific session of 'sound' work as a warm up or as a valuable learning activity in its own right.

Resources

a mirror large enough for the child to see his/her own face and yours, drinking straws, paper shapes, raisins/small sweets, 'hundreds and thousands', jam or chocolate spread, lollies, lipstick or face paint, feathers, cotton wool balls, cotton buds, paper tissues, wooden lolly sticks or spatulas, thread, ping-pong ball, bubbles, a saucer, tongue book (make using Figures 4.1 and 4.2), facial expressions pictures (Figure 4.3), record sheets (e.g. Figure 4.4)

Make yourself a 'kit' so that you or your teaching assistant can select one or two activities for each session and everything is at hand.

Figure 4.1 Tongue book pictures

© Gill Thompson (2003) *Supporting Communication Disorders*, David Fulton Publishers.

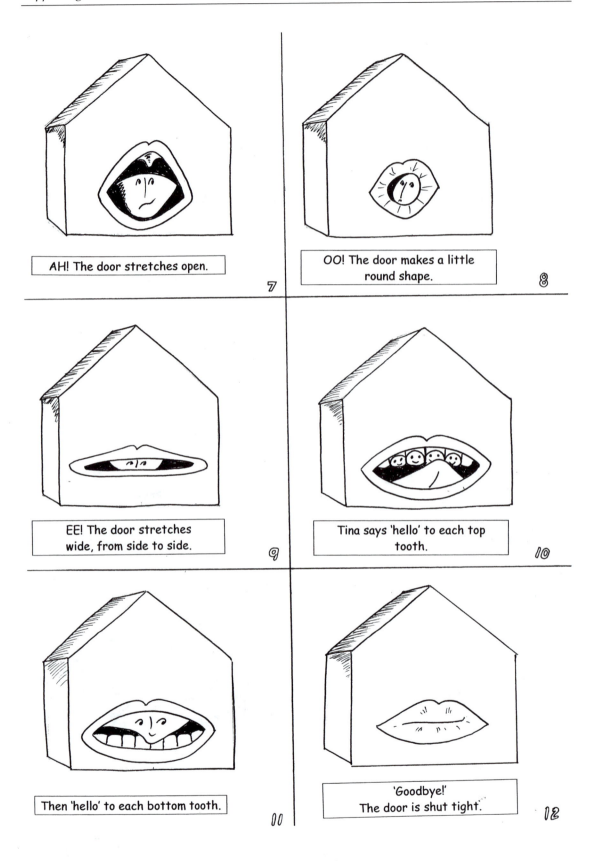

Figure 4.2 Tongue book pictures

© Gill Thompson (2003) *Supporting Communication Disorders*, David Fulton Publishers.

Expressions

Figure 4.3   Facial expressions

© Gill Thompson (2003) *Supporting Communication Disorders*, David Fulton Publishers.

Programme of activities – sensory awareness

From the following list select two or three activities to carry out with the child so that the programme changes each day. You may choose to use the record sheet provided (Figure 4.4) to note which activities have been used and how the child responded.

1. Using the tongue book (make using the photocopiable resource, Figures 4.1 and 4.2) encourage the child to imitate the lip and tongue shapes. The mirror can be used to provide visual reinforcement. Make a note of difficult tongue positions as these can be reinforced by other activities.
2. Using the 'expressions' pictures (Figure 4.3), encourage the child to imitate the facial expressions. This is also an opportunity to talk about the different expressions and what feelings they show.
3. Place a dab of jam or chocolate spread on the child's lip in a single position (use a cotton bud or wooden lolly stick) and ask the child to lick it off. The mirror is useful for this, providing visual feedback.
4. Encourage the child to lick all the way round their lips. Model the movement so the child can imitate.
5. Hold the lolly in front of the child's mouth and ask him/her to lick it – at the top, at the bottom, up and down etc. Make sure the tongue moves and not the lolly! You may need to demonstrate this!
6. Sprinkle a few 'hundreds and thousands' on a saucer and encourage the child to lick them up with the tip of the tongue.
7. Tie a feather (the fluffy ones are best) to a thread and let it hang in front of the child's mouth. Ask the child to blow it away. Later on in the programme, maintain the blowing so the feather stays away for as long as possible.
8. Play a blowing game using a straw:
   Blow a small piece of tissue paper or a cotton ball across the table.
   Play 'blow football' using a ping-pong ball and a playing field sheet – best played on a tray with raised sides (two children can compete).
   Blow bubbles into a glass of water using the straw.
9. Play sucking games with a straw:
   Suck up coloured pieces of paper (brightly coloured gummed shapes are useful) on the end of the straw and then drop them into a pot.
   Suck up a raisin or small sweet and see how many the child can collect (this can be done as a group game).
   Suck a thick liquid through the straw, e.g. thick milkshake, fruit puree.
10. Blow bubbles using a wand and soapy liquid.
11. Keeping lips firmly closed, blow out the cheeks and then push the cheeks to blow a 'raspberry'.
12. Put lipstick on the lips and then make a lip pattern by pressing lips on to a tissue or piece of paper.

Talk about the activity with the child. If they find it difficult, show them what to do and touch the relevant part of the lip or tongue with a clean straw or spatula.

Making Sounds – Activity Record

Name: D.o.b./Age:

Activity	1	2	3	4	5	6	7
Tongue book							
Pulling faces							
Licking jam							
Licking all round lips							
Licking a lolly							
Licking 'hundreds and thousands'							
Blowing a feather							
Blow football (or similar)							
Blowing bubbles in water							
Blowing bubbles with a wand							
Sucking games (paper pieces, sweets etc.)							
Sucking a thick liquid							
Blowing a 'raspberry'							
Lipstick patterns							
Listening to taped sounds							
Listening to sound makers							
Listening – single speech sounds							
Listening – initial sounds							
Listening – final sounds							
Listening – difference between two sounds							

Figure 4.4   Making sounds – activity record sheet

© Gill Thompson (2003) *Supporting Communication Disorders*, David Fulton Publishers.

Activities to introduce basic listening skills

Programme of activities – listening games

These activities are intended to encourage the child to listen to sounds and discriminate between them. There are two main aims involved:

- to increase awareness of different initial consonant sounds;
- to help the child discriminate between similar sounds.

If you are working with a very young child, they are unlikely to recognise the written letter shapes. This can become a teaching exercise to reinforce the learning of letter shapes being taught in class or, you may choose to use pictures. If the child confuses specific sounds and substitutes one for the other (uses /t/ for /f/ or /f/ for /th/) you can adapt the activity accordingly.

1. Identifying non-speech sounds

There are several commercial listening activities using cassettes with animal sounds, sounds of vehicles, sounds around the home etc. These are a good starting point to encourage the child to listen and match a sound to a picture.

You can also use a variety of sound-making objects – a bell, a drum, a shaker, crumpled paper, a spoon in a cup, a whistle, a kazoo, a squeaky toy etc. Introduce these objects to the child first, at the start of the activity. After this the child should not be able to see what you are using to make the sound, so hide the objects behind a cloth or screen. Depending on the child's communication skills, you can ask them to tell you what you used or you can provide picture cards for the child to choose from (see sound makers pictures in Figure 4.5).

2. Listening for the correct single speech sound

Practise a particular sound with the child so that you are sure that they know the sound. The child may not be able to produce it correctly at this stage. Use a screen or large book between you and the child so that they cannot see your mouth. Give them a selection of easily recognisable pictures (start with just two or three pictures) and ask the child to point to or pick up the one that you say starting with a . . . /s/ (or whichever sound you are working on). For example 'Which one am I saying?' and show them pictures of

sun, gun, bun   mitt, sit, hit   tea, sea, pea

(see Figure 4.6). This activity can be used for all single initial sounds. For older children you can use word cards instead of pictures.

Sound makers

Figure 4.5 Sound makers

Auditory discrimination pictures

Figure 4.6 Auditory discrimination pictures

© Gill Thompson (2003) *Supporting Communication Disorders*, David Fulton Publishers.

A similar game can be played to identify final consonants, for example

present pictures of: bus, bug, bun   hit, hill, hiss   cat, cap, can.

3. Hearing the difference between two similar sounds (p/b, s/sh, t/d, k/g)

Give the child pairs of picture cards (see examples on picture pair sheet, Figure 4.7). The child should listen and decide which word you have said.

pear/bear   pea/bee   pin/bin   pail/bale   pie/bye,   etc.

4. Initial sounds

Give the child two letter cards with an associated picture to provide a visual prompt. Say a word clearly and the child has to guess which letter/sound the word begins with.

For example f/th

fish, fat, fall, full, fan, fin, fee, face, fair, fun
this, that, than, thin, the, there, thumb

These are just a few ideas for you to consider. You may want to develop and adapt some of the suggestions to suit a specific child's needs.

Multisensory teaching

If you link the teaching of sounds with the recognition of letter shapes and writing the letters it may help to use a multisensory approach. Plastic or sandpaper letters provide a sensory experience of the 'feel' of the letter shapes.

1. Encourage the child to trace over the letter with index and middle finger, following the correct direction for writing the letter.
2. The child can then 'draw' the letter in a sand tray with one finger.
3. Draw the letter really large in the air, using the whole arm.
4. Then use a pencil or crayon to write the letter on paper.

Modelling clay or playdough can be used to make the letter of the alphabet that is being worked on. This provides additional reinforcement of the letter shape. Pictograms can also give additional clues to help the child remember the letter shape – /s/ can become a snake, /b/ can be made from a bat and ball, /c/ can be drawn as the handle on a cup etc.

Picture pairs

pear/bear

pea/bee

pin/bin

pail/bale

pie/bye

Figure 4.7 Picture pairs

© Gill Thompson (2003) *Supporting Communication Disorders*, David Fulton Publishers.

5 Articulation – ideas for teaching specific sounds

When you have completed your evaluation of the child's speech and have identified the sounds that are deviant, you will want to incorporate some intervention strategies into your planning. Plan your programme realistically – it takes time to learn or re-learn sounds and even longer to establish them in everyday speech. If a speech and language therapist is seeing the child, ask advice on developing a programme of reinforcement for the classroom. You do not want to confuse the child by working on different sounds to those being addressed during therapy. If the child is awaiting therapy or has not been referred, select a sound that is going to be your focus and plan a simple progressive programme, which can be delivered in a one-to-one situation for a few minutes each day. If this is to be done by the SENCO or a teaching assistant, the class teacher should be kept aware of progress so that further reinforcement can be done in the classroom, perhaps as part of the phonics or reading sessions.

The sounds that you have assessed and are likely to want to work on are consonants. Vowel sounds are less likely to be produced incorrectly and, if they are, you will need to seek advice from the speech and language therapist for working on them.

Speech book

I usually make a 'speech book' for the child. I duplicate each activity (copied sheets to go in a folder) to give parents an opportunity to reinforce the sounds at home. The book is updated every couple of weeks with new pictures and provides a record of progress and a way of revising. It also shows the class teacher what we are working on. I draw or stick pictures into the book, add photos from the school digital camera, make opening windows or flaps to reveal a picture, provide simple board games, envelopes of pictures etc. so that the book is very personal to the child. Figure 5.1 shows pages from a speech book depicting activities for the sound /s/.

Speech book – suggestions for activities for the sound 's'

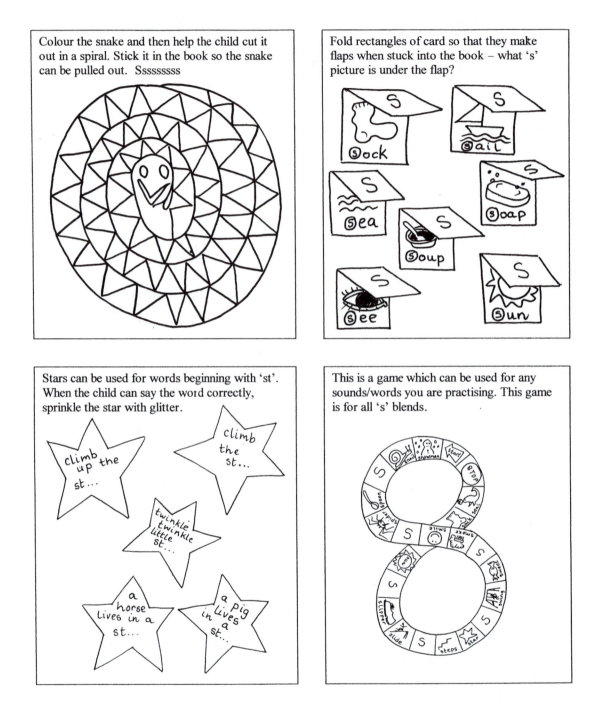

Colour the snake and then help the child cut it out in a spiral. Stick it in the book so the snake can be pulled out. Sssssssss

Fold rectangles of card so that they make flaps when stuck into the book – what 's' picture is under the flap?

Stars can be used for words beginning with 'st'. When the child can say the word correctly, sprinkle the star with glitter.

This is a game which can be used for any sounds/words you are practising. This game is for all 's' blends.

Figure 5.1 Examples of pages from a speech book

Progressive formula for introducing sound

As a general rule for introducing a sound follow this progressive formula:

1. Each sound is taught *in isolation* using games to encourage the child to make the sound correctly. Encourage the child to watch your mouth and tongue movements and imitate. Use a mirror to reinforce this. With young children it is helpful to associate a sound with a picture of things that make the sound.

    p – a fish blowing bubbles – p, p, p
    b – a bouncing ball – b, b, b
    t – a dripping tap – t, t, t
    d – drumsticks on a drum – dd, dd, dd
    s – a hissing snake – sssssssss
    z – a buzzing bee – zzzzzzzz
    f – a rabbit with his front teeth over his bottom lip – ffffff
    v – a plane engine as it flies in the sky – vvvvvvvvv
    sh – finger to lips – shhhhhh
    r – a roaring lion – rrrrrr
    l – singing – la, la, la

2. Use the sound *in nonsense syllables* (use Figure 5.2, the balloon sheet). Write each of the nonsense syllables beginning with the target sound in a balloon and play a game pretending to 'pop' each balloon and saying the sound as it 'pops'.

    pah, pay, pee, paw, pow, poh, poo
    bah, bay, bee, baw, bow, boh, boo
    fah, fay, fee, faw, fow, foh, foo
    tah, tay, tee, taw, tow, toh, too
    dah, day, dee, daw, dow, doh, doo
    sah, say, see, saw, sow, soh, soo
    lah, lay, lee, law, low, loh, loo
    kah, kay, kee, kaw, kow, koh, koo
    gah, gay, gee, gaw, gow, goh, goo

3. Use the sound *in an initial position* in simple c-v-c (consonant-vowel-consonant) words that can be easily drawn. Use the pure sound – *do not introduce consonant blends yet*. Concentrate on the specific sound you are working on – do not worry about how the rest of the word is produced for the moment.

    /p/ – pig, pan, pin, pot, pad, post, pie, pea etc.
    /b/ – bat, ball, bin, bus, bow, bun, bed, bell etc.
    /f/ – fish, fin, face, foot, feet, fan, four, five etc.
    /t/ – tea, top, tap, tin, tail, tie, toe etc.
    /d/ – dog, door, dig, duck, dish, dark etc.
    /s/ – sun, sea, sack, see-saw, sail, sand, soap, soup etc.
    /l/ – lip, lock, lick, leaf, light, lamp, laugh etc.
    /k/ – car, cup, cat, cap, cot, coat, key, king, etc.*
    /g/ – gun, gate, ghost, girl etc.

* (Use words beginning with /k/ or /c/ as it is the sound you are teaching and not the letter shape – although the two different letter shapes can be pointed out.)

Figure 5.2 Balloons

© Gill Thompson (2003) *Supporting Communication Disorders*, David Fulton Publishers.

4. Introduce the sound *in final word positions* in simple c-v-c words.
   /p/ – cap, cup, tip, tap, top, hop, mop, ship etc.
   /b/ – rub, tub, pub, knob, bob etc.
   /f/ – fluff, stiff, sniff, cuff, puff, laugh etc.
   /t/ – sit, hot, hut, mat, mitt, pot, cot, cat, fat, wet, kite etc.
   /d/ – lid, hide, ride, wide, pod, sad, red etc.
   /s/ – bus, kiss, horse, race, face, mess, dress etc.
   /l/ – ball, bell, fall, call, wall, well, till, tall, mill, doll etc.
   /k/ – duck, sock, sack, rock, cake, bake, rake etc.
   /g/ – rug, slug, mug, big, wig, dig, bag etc.

5. Teach the sound *in medial positions*. These can be difficult to hear so you
   may find it easier to split the word into two parts so the sound is actually
   an initial or final sound. Where the word is split will depend on the
   sound you are working on.

racing (ray – sing)	stopping (stop – ing)	rubber (rub – er)
rocket (rock – et)	digging (dig – ing)	butter (but – er)
ladder (lad – er)	welly (well – ee)	coffee (cof – ee)

6. Only move on to initial *consonant blends* when the child has managed to
   consistently make the sound in all word positions. If the child is having
   problems with other sounds you may want to wait until both of the
   consonants are established before blending them together. Practise
   each blend one at a time. Pictures can be useful for this activity as
   shown in Figure 5.3 for consonant blends with /s/.

   sk, sl, sp, sm, sn, st – skip, slug, spoon, smell, snow, star
   pl, pr – plug, prince
   kl, kr – clock, cream
   tr, tw – tree, twig
   fl, fr – flag, frog
   bl, br – blue, bright
   gl, gr – glove, grow
   dr – drink, draw, drive, dress

7. When the sound is well established in single words, build two- to three-
   word *phrases, sentences* and *simple tongue twisters*. Develop stories that
   incorporate the sound or find pictures to describe using the sound in
   spontaneous speech.

   six socks
   Sam saw six horses at the seaside.
   Sally sat on a stool and a spider sat beside her.

I have suggested articulation programmes for introducing and teaching
/s/, /k/, /th/, /sh/, /f/ and /p/ (see activity sheets in Figures 5.4 to 5.9).
You can adapt the same format for any consonant that the child finds difficult
and substitute appropriate words to match your selected sound.

Pictures for consonant blend 's' – sn, sl, sp, sm, st

Figure 5.3 Pictures for /s/ blends

© Gill Thompson (2003) *Supporting Communication Disorders*, David Fulton Publishers.

ARTICULATION	Ideas for the /s/ sound

/s/ is often misarticulated. If left uncorrected, it can persist into adulthood as a 'lisp'.
The sound /s/ may become /th/ if the tongue is placed too close to the teeth.
The sound is also produced within the high frequency range and children with a hearing difficulty (or who have had intermittent hearing loss) may find this sound difficult to discriminate and produce. The /s/ sound can be written in several ways and this will need to be pointed out to an older child – bu**s**, ki**ss**, hou**s**e, i**ce**.

1. Introduce the sound
A snake is the natural choice as an image for /s/ but you could use a picture of air escaping from a balloon or tyre or a firework whistling through the air. Begin by teaching the **sound in isolation**, showing how to place the tongue behind the top front teeth.

Use a mirror to reinforce visually and, if necessary, a straw to touch the area on the palate immediately behind the teeth. The child who finds this difficult will need to do **tongue exercises** to become more aware of tongue placement and may find it helpful to hold a straw up against the roof of the mouth with their tongue and try blowing air down the straw . . . it is worth a try!

2. Auditory discrimination activities should be done to ensure that the child can hear the sound – give the child some cards with a snake on them and say a string of individual sounds. When the child hears /s/ they give you a snake card. Or you could have a puppet snake which the child 'feeds' with a counter every time a /s/ is heard.
Move on to words with an initial /s/ when the child can hear the sound in isolation.

3. Teach /s/ in initial positions

sea, sun, sand, soap, soup, sum, suck, sail, seal, sew, sit

You can then go on to the voiced sound /z/: (picture – a bee buzzing), zoo, zip, zebra

4. Teach /s/ in a final position

bus, kiss, mess, horse, face, race, mouse, mice, dice, ice
(/z/ can also be taught: has, is, was, rose, nose, hose)

5. Medial /s/
messy, kissing, hissing, racing, crossing
(/z/: buzzing, lazy, roses)

6. Introduce the /s/ blends one at a time and be aware that the sound it is blended with could also be difficult for the child.

spoon, spade, speak, spot
smile, smoke, small
snow, snail, snake, snap
skip, skate, skull
sleep, slide, slow, slipper
step, stop, sting, stick, stone
swing, sweet, swan, swim

7. Begin using phrases and rhymes to encourage use in continuous speech.

See the sun in the sky?   This soup is so good.   Sit on a stool.
Sing a song of sixpence.   Six silly swans swimming in the sea.

8. Monitor the child's ability to use the /s/ and /z/ sounds in spontaneous speech.

Figure 5.4 Articulation sheet /s/

© Gill Thompson (2003) *Supporting Communication Disorders*, David Fulton Publishers.

ARTICULATION	Ideas for the /k/c/ sound

The sound /k/c/ is often omitted or replaced by another sound. This is partly because it is made at the back of the mouth and so cannot be seen by the child and partly because, if there is any reduction in hearing acuity, it may sound similar to other consonants. This sound can also be confusing as it is represented by both /c/ and /k/ - point this out to the child using a descriptive image, i.e. 'curly /c/ and kicking /k/'.

1. Auditory discrimination – between /k/ and the chosen substitute sound
Use pictures and work with pairs of words (e.g. /t/ may be the substitute sound):

car/tar   key/tea   cake/take   come/tum   call/tall   cap/tap

Say one of the words and ask the child to indicate the picture of the word you said. Alternatively, give the child a pair of letter cards k and t and ask them to point to the sound they hear at the beginning of the word. They could have a pile of each letter card and post the relevant card into a postbox.

2. Begin by teaching the sound in isolation
Explain how the sounds are made – /t/ is made at the front of the mouth and /k/ is right at the back (draw a picture of a train to illustrate this idea). The child should place a counter at the front or back of the train when they hear a /t/ or a /k/.

Call /t/ a 'front' sound and /k/ a 'back' sound.

Ask the child to feel your throat as you make the sound and then to feel their own throat as they attempt to produce kkkk. It is sometimes easier to make the /k/ sound if the child lies on their back – try this if all else fails.
Use a picture for the /k/ sound – a gun firing, an engine starting up, a bird making a 'caw-caw' sound.
Once the child has successfully produced the sound, use it in simple nonsense syllables – kah, kay, kee etc.

3. Initial word position
Practise simple c-v-c words beginning with /k/ or /c/ using pictures and games.

car, cat, cap, cup, can, cot, come, cut, key, king

4. Final word position
Introduce words which end in the /k/ sound (point out to the child that both k and c are sometimes used together in this position).

back, sick, rock, pack, tick, sock, sack, kick, bark, dark

5. Medial position

bucket, rocket, pocket, parking, picking, ticket

6. Initial blends

cl – clock, clown, clap, clean, class, climb
cr – cry, crow, crack, crawl, crust, cream

7. Continuous speech
Reinforce and encourage the correct use of /k/ in phrases and sentences:

I can count quickly.   Can you catch the kite?   Kim cooked a cake.
The king counted his coins in the counting house.   a cup of coffee
Catch a crab.   Katy is kicking the can.   Come and call the cows.

Figure 5.5   Articulation sheet /k/c/

© Gill Thompson (2003) *Supporting Communication Disorders*, David Fulton Publishers.

| ARTICULATION | Ideas for the /th/ sound |

/th/ is a sound which is often misarticulated. If left uncorrected, it can persist into adulthood.

The sound /f/ is frequently used as a substitute for /th/ and /v/ instead of the voiced sound /th/. There may be confusion between /s/ and /th/. /s/ may become /th/ if the tongue is placed too close to the teeth.

Difficulties with reading can arise from the wrong pronunciation of this sound and, in an older child, speech will sound immature if /th/ is said as /f/ or /v/.

It may help to use the tongue and lip exercises as an introduction to this sound.

1. **Auditory discrimination** activities should be done to ensure that the child can hear the difference between /th/ and /f/.

that/fat   thin/fin   thaw/four   (three/free throw/fro)

2. Begin by teaching the **sound in isolation**, showing how to place the tongue between top and bottom teeth. Use a mirror to reinforce visually, a finger to touch the tongue as it emerges. The child who finds this difficult will need to do **tongue exercises** to become more aware of tongue placement.

3. **Teach /th/ in initial positions**. Be aware that there are two ways of saying /th/ - th as in **thin** and th as in **that** (voiceless/voiced). Teach the voiceless sound first.

thin, thick, thistle, thumb, thank, thorn   thumb →

You can then go on to the voiced sound: that, this, then, the, those etc.

4. **Teach /th/ in a final position**

bath, path, with, heath, breath, sheath, tooth, teeth

5. **Medial /th/ is usually voiced**

mother, father, brother, feather, weather, leather, heather, bother

6. **Introduce the /thr/ cluster**

three, throat, thrush, thread, bathroom

7. **Begin using phrases and rhymes to encourage use in continuous speech.**
Three thorns in my thumb.
There are thirty thousand feathers on a thrush's throat.
The path led through the heather.
Whether the weather is hot or whether the weather is not, we'll weather the weather whatever the weather, whether we like it or not!

8. **Monitor the child's ability to discriminate the f/v/th sounds.**

Figure 5.6 Articulation sheet /th/

ARTICULATION	Ideas for the /sh/ sound (and /ch/)

Children often find /sh/ difficult and may confuse it with /s/.
The sounds /s/ and /sh/ are very close, both in the tongue placement and in the frequency level for hearing. Children with a hearing difficulty (or who have had intermittent hearing loss) may find this sound difficult to discriminate and produce.

1. Introduce the sound
A picture of a face with a finger in front of the mouth can be used as a visual image. You could also use a shell as a visual prompt – the child could listen for the 'sh' of the sea in a large shell.
Begin by teaching the **sound in isolation**, showing how to place the tongue behind the top front teeth and pushing out the air to make a 'shushing' sound.
Use a mirror to reinforce visually and, if necessary, a straw to touch the area on the palate immediately behind the teeth. The child who finds this difficult will need to do **tongue exercises** to become more aware of tongue placement and may find it helpful to hold a straw up against the roof of the mouth with their tongue and try blowing air out around the straw. This sound differs from /s/ in that the air escapes over a wider area at the front of the tongue.

2. Auditory discrimination activities should be done to ensure that the child can hear the sound – give the child some cards with a snake on one for /s/ and the clown face on the other for /sh/.
Say the following words and see if the child can tell which sound you are saying at the beginning of the word:

> sigh/shy, seep/sheep, sew/show, sop/shop,
> sake/shake, sun/shun, saw/shore etc.

Move on to words with an initial /sh/ when the child can hear the sound in isolation and hear the difference between /s/ and /sh/.

3. Teach /sh/ in initial positions

> ship, shop, sheep, show, shake, shark, shoe, shell

4. Teach /sh/ in a final position

> fish, dish, wash, splash, rush, push, bush

5. Medial /sh/

> washing, machine, fishing, dishes, fishes, cushion, seashell

6. Begin using phrases and rhymes to encourage use in continuous speech and to use both /sh/ and /s/ together.

> she can see the ship   sea shells on the sea shore
> put the washing in the washing machine
> the shark swam slowly to the sandy shore
> the fish shook his fin and splashed the fisherman

7. Monitor the child's ability to use /sh/ and /s/ correctly in spontaneous speech.

You could also introduce /ch/, which has a similar articulation pattern to /sh/ but the tongue makes a 'tap' against the roof of the mouth. Use a train as a prompt for this sound.

> chip, chop, cheek, chair, cheese
> catch, witch, touch, hop-scotch, torch, church, patch
> patches, scratching, catching, itchy

You can move on to the 'j' sound, which is made in the same way as /ch/ but with voicing.

> jam, jelly, jump, jug
> hedge, sledge, fudge, ledge, badge
> badger, sledging, Roger

Figure 5.7 Articulation sheet /sh/ and /ch/

© Gill Thompson (2003) *Supporting Communication Disorders*, David Fulton Publishers.

> **ARTICULATION** Ideas for the /f/, /v/ sound

/f/ is often confused with /th/ and substituted for it. Some children, however, do not make the /f/ sound correctly and need to learn it.

1. Introduce the sound
A rabbit with its two front teeth sticking out, demonstrates the correct position for making the sound. Make a headband with two large ears to complete the image for a very young child.

Begin by teaching the **sound in isolation**, showing how to place the top front teeth gently over the lower lip and blowing air out gently and continuously.

Use a mirror to reinforce the sound visually.

2. Auditory discrimination activities should be done so that the child is able to hear and recognise /f/ in isolation, in nonsense syllables and at the beginning of c-v-c words.
Use the balloon sheet (Figure 5.2) to teach the sound in syllables – fee, fah, foo, fay, fow, foh.

You could also introduce the voiced sound /v/ and do some work on this, listening to the difference between f/v in words like fan/van, fat/vat.

3. Teach /f/ in initial positions

   fat, fan, fin, fit, fish, face, four, five, fall, foot, phone
   (van, vet, vase, vote)

4. Teach /f/ in a final position

   laugh, rough, sniff, cough, stiff
   (have, five, live, hive, move, dove, love, shave, brave)

5. Medial /f/

   coffee, toffee, laughing, stuffing
   (cover, having, over, shaving)

6. Introduce /f/ blends one at a time – if the child has difficulty making /r/ and /l/ you may first need to work on these sounds before blending them together.

   /fl/ fly, flap, flower, flow, flash
   /fr/ fry, fresh, frock, free, frog

7. Begin using phrases and rhymes to encourage the use of /f/ in continuous speech.

   four fat fish   Fanny's face   fit five feathers on the fence
   five fat frogs had four fish for tea   fresh flowers fit in a full vase

8. Monitor the child's ability to use the /f/ and /v/ sounds in spontaneous speech.

Figure 5.8 Articulation sheet /f/, /v/

© Gill Thompson (2003) *Supporting Communication Disorders*, David Fulton Publishers.

ARTICULATION	Ideas for the /p/, /b/ sound

/p/ and /b/ are fairly straightforward sounds to introduce as they are made at the front of the mouth and the lip closure is easily visible. Children who have difficulty with closing their lips firmly may struggle to build up air to puff out. It would be helpful to do the tongue and lip exercises as a starting point to working on this sound, particularly the blowing and sucking activities and making lipstick prints on paper.

Many children do not hear the difference in voicing between /p/ and /b/ so you may need to work on listening skills.

1. Introduce the sound

A balloon popping can provide a good visual image for this sound.

You may also want to show the child that they need to close their lips tightly. Use a mirror to reinforce the sound visually.

Begin by teaching the **sound in isolation**.

2. Auditory Discrimination activities should be done so that the child is able to hear and recognise /p/ in isolation, in nonsense syllables and at the beginning of c-v-c words.

Use the balloon sheet (Figure 5.2) to teach the sound in syllables – pee, pah, poo, pay, pow, poh.

You can also introduce the voiced sound /b/ and do some work on this, listening to the difference between p/b in syllables and words like pea/bee, pat/bat, pin/bin.

3. Teach /p/ in initial positions

> pat, pan, pen, pin, pit, paw, pot, pet, pill, pull
> (bat, bin, bit, bike, ball, bun, bed, bear)

4. Teach /p/ in a final position

> tap, top, hop, cap, ship, shop, shape, rope
> (tub, knob, cab, rub, web)

5. Medial /p/

> happy, nappy, puppy, hopping, shopping, clapping, tapping, pepper
> (baby, label, table, rubber)

6. Introduce /p/ blends one at a time – if the child has difficulty making /r/ and /l/ you may first need to work on these sounds before blending them together.

> **/pl/** play, plate, place, please, plug, plus
> **/bl/** blow, black, blue, blood, blink
> **/pr/** pram, pray, prize, prune
> **/br/** brick, bread, break, broom, brown, brush

7. Begin using phrases and rhymes to encourage the use of /p/ in continuous speech.

pop the pin up on the top   pack the peas in the pot
put the puppy on the porch   Peter put pepper on the plate of potatoes
Betty bought a big bag of buns   Ben the bear blows bubbles

8. Monitor the child's ability to use the /p/ and /b/ sounds in spontaneous speech.

Figure 5.9 Articulation sheet /p/, /b/

6 Language – assessment and ideas for intervention programmes

What is language?

Language is the ability to understand and use a structured system of sounds and words for communication. It is a component of the whole process of learning and is essential for accessing every aspect of the school curriculum. If a child has a language difficulty, it is likely to impact on everything that they do, in every facet of their lives. Difficulties are not always easy to identify and, if the disorder is not accompanied by unclear speech, the child may be labelled as inattentive, slow to learn or just lazy. Speech and language therapists use the term 'language' in a slightly different way to teachers. To a teacher, language development is the overall term for developing reading, spelling and language concepts. To a therapist, language development is the fundamental interrelationship between linguistic skills, enabling a child to communicate beyond the stage of labelling objects.

All aspects of the speech and language 'chain' of development are closely related so that difficulties with the production of speech sounds can influence the development of linguistic concepts.

Early language development is linked with the development of cognitive, social and communication skills. Central to the development of language are the child's ability to focus attention, to learn through play and to form social interactions.

Language difficulties in children need to be considered in various ways:

Language delay – the child's language development may be immature but following a normal pattern.

Language disorder – development is atypical or sufficiently delayed to suggest that there may be an underlying pathological or neurological cause (see Chapter 8).

The two main aspects of language are often categorised as receptive language skills and expressive language skills.

Receptive language

Receptive language skills concern the child's ability to understand and process language. Difficulties in this area can be the result of auditory or listening difficulties, a poor auditory memory, sequencing difficulties, difficulties processing the components of language, i.e. vocabulary and grammar. Children with difficulty processing language will frequently have problems with auditory retention/auditory memory (holding on to auditory information in order to follow an instruction or fully understand verbal explanations) and limited comprehension of essential basic concepts.

As language skills are acquired, we use them to organise our thoughts and to reason. Children who have not developed good language skills may have problems with verbal reasoning and making sense of the huge amount of information that is part of everyday life. Some children will find it difficult to understand beyond the literal, misinterpreting colloquial speech and missing jokes and inferences. These are the children who most need additional explanations, visual prompts and support to follow a task in small progressive steps. They are also the children who are least likely to ask for help or to admit that they have not understood. They may try to carry out a given task without really understanding what to do, in an attempt to at least produce something for the teacher. This can lead to low self-esteem, withdrawal or, conversely, avoidance techniques and behaviour problems.

Expressive language

Expressive language skills concern the production and use of language and language structures. A child with difficulties in this area may use limited or inappropriate vocabulary. Sentence structure may be slow to develop, unusual in the way words are strung together or confused in content. The child may have poor social communication skills, be unable to recognise when to speak, how to respond to questions, how to take part in a conversation or how to interact verbally in different situations. They may appear immature, withdrawn, attention seeking or even rude.

Children are likely to present with a combination of these two aspects of language since the two are so closely linked (Figure 6.1). However, there may be a predominance of either a **receptive** or **expressive** disorder. In order to assess language, it is helpful to identify which specific areas are affected and then address these individually. You may find that the child has a combination of several factors, but by breaking down the overall language profile into areas, it makes it easier to plan a manageable programme of intervention.

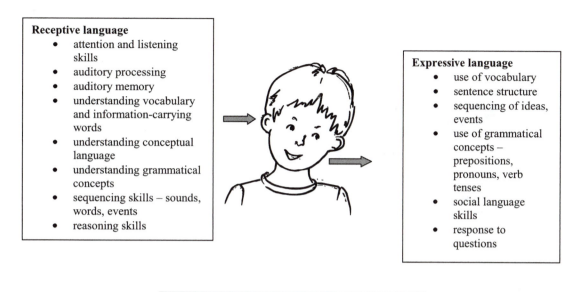

Receptive language
- attention and listening skills
- auditory processing
- auditory memory
- understanding vocabulary and information-carrying words
- understanding conceptual language
- understanding grammatical concepts
- sequencing skills – sounds, words, events
- reasoning skills

Expressive language
- use of vocabulary
- sentence structure
- sequencing of ideas, events
- use of grammatical concepts – prepositions, pronouns, verb tenses
- social language skills
- response to questions

Receptive and expressive language skills

Figure 6.1 Receptive and expressive language

Assessing receptive language skills (understanding)

Vocabulary

Test/investigate the child's:

- ability to understand single word labels – use objects or pictures – 'show me the . . .' (an assessment such as *The British Picture Vocabulary Scale* (Dunn *et al.* 1997, see Resources) can provide a good idea of the level of understanding and also gives age equivalence);
- ability to understand action words – use pictures or actions;
- understanding of basic concepts – colour, size, position etc.

Following verbal instructions

This will relate to the child's ability to recall and process auditory information, for example:

- a simple instruction – 'Give me the ball' when offering a choice of different objects;
- a two-part instruction – 'Give me the red ball' when offering a choice of different coloured objects (a red ball, a red pencil, a blue ball, a blue pencil, a yellow ball, a yellow pencil);
- more complex instructions – 'Get me the book and the box from the table next door. Then you can go on the computer.' Children may not be able to deal with several concepts at once. They may only process key words from a verbal instruction, homing in on certain 'information-carrying words', which will limit their overall understanding (see Figure 6.2).

49

Auditory processing
The child may only retain fragments of verbal information and be unable to process the whole instruction.

Figure 6.2 Auditory processing

Listening skills and attention span

These are essential learning tools for developing language skills, taking in information, and understanding what to do.

- Share a simple story and then see if the child has been able to remember the main events and characters.
- Observe the child during story time or at the introductory part of a lesson – note lapses in attention, attempts to divert others, inappropriate comments or behaviour.
- Monitor the child's need to pick up clues from other children about what to do.

Understanding of grammar

We often assume that a child is understanding more than he or she actually does. They may be getting the gist of a sentence or phrase without really being able to decode the more complex structures within it. Investigate the child's understanding of:

- plurals (use cards or pictures such as those in Figure 6.3 – one cat/several cats, a man/men);
- tenses (questions about what the child is doing now, what they did yesterday – related pictures – I am playing football, I played football, I am painting a picture, I painted a picture);
- negatives – he is eating, he isn't eating, it is raining, it is not raining (e.g. use Figure 6.4);
- prepositions – using a sheet such as Figure 6.5 position the ball – in the box, behind the box, beside the box, between the boxes, under the box;
- pronouns – match phrases to pictures – he is running, she is running, they are running;
- questions – Who? What? Where? When? Why?

Sequencing

This can be putting the words in the right order to make sense, remembering the main events in a story and sequencing them correctly, dealing with time sequences or dealing with two-part instructions. To investigate sequencing:

- Show picture cards that build a sequence, tell the story and then mix up the cards and ask the child 'Which comes first? Which comes next? What happened at the end?' Can the child order the events?
- Talk about an everyday event like putting on clothes – give the child pictures of different clothes and a boy or girl to dress – can the child sort out what order to dress the boy/girl in?

Language assessment pictures – plurals

Show me . . . 'cat'

cat/cats

Show me . . . 'men'

man/men

Show me . . . 'balloons'

balloon/balloons

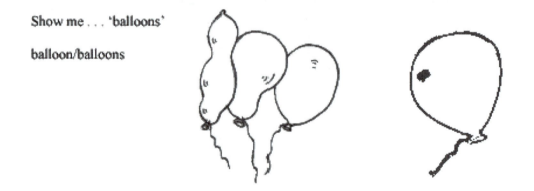

Figure 6.3 Language assessment pictures – plurals

© Gill Thompson (2003) *Supporting Communication Disorders*, David Fulton Publishers.

Language assessment pictures – negatives

Show me . . . 'not raining'

Show me . . . 'not sitting'

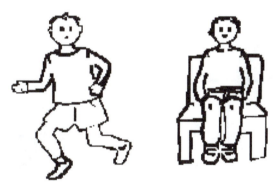

Show me . . . 'not eating'

Figure 6.4   Language assessment pictures – negatives

© Gill Thompson (2003) *Supporting Communication Disorders*, David Fulton Publishers.

Language assessment pictures – prepositions

Show me . . . the ball in the box . . . the ball behind the box . . . the ball on the box . . . the ball under the box . . . the ball in front of the box . . . the ball next to the box

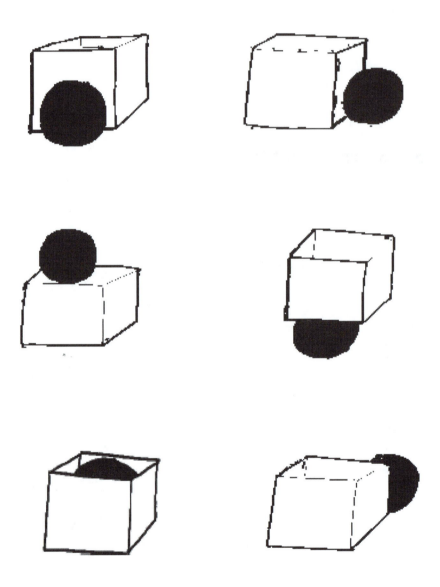

Figure 6.5   Language assessment pictures – prepositions

© Gill Thompson (2003) *Supporting Communication Disorders*, David Fulton Publishers.

Assessing expressive language skills (output)

To evaluate a child's expressive ability and use of language it is helpful to set up an informal play situation and tape-record a sample of the child's speech. This will allow you to analyse the content at a later time and you will find that you will pick out the problems more easily. The sample of speech could involve talking about pictures, responding to questions, role-play or inter-action with a puppet or toy. Look for use of vocabulary, sentence formation, appropriate responses to questions, use of verbs and tenses, pronouns etc. Is the child's expressive language used appropriately to convey meaning, indicate the child's needs, communicate feelings and relate experiences?

Ideas for support and intervention programmes

Complete the 'Language Assessment Record' (Figure 6.6) to provide a profile of the child's ability to understand and use language. Where there are areas of weakness, you can plan activities to teach and practise these specific skills. This could involve the teaching of basic concepts such as colour, position, shape, number values etc. or could be at a more advanced stage, working on the use of pronouns, plurals or verb tenses. Activities can be incorporated into whole-class teaching or used as the focus of small group activities.

Use a variety of activities to encourage the use of language and thinking skills. There are many commercially produced resources such as 'What's Wrong?' cards, 'Sequential Thinking' cards, story sequences etc. (all available from LDA, see Resources list). Targets can be written into the child's IEP with clear criteria for success.

Language Assessment Record

Name: Age/D.o.b.:

Date of assessment: (✓ to indicate child's ability)

Receptive language (understanding)	
Understands single word labels	
Understands basic concepts: Colours Shapes Position words (in, on, under, in front of, behind)	
Understands action words : running, sitting, jumping, riding	
Follows simple (one-part) instructions	
Follows two-part instructions	
Follows complex, multi-part instructions	
Understands plurals: man/men cat/ cats toy/toys	
Understands negatives: is not, can't, won't	
Understands pronouns: me, you, him/her, we, they	
Understands question words: What? When? Who? Where?	
Can sort objects/pictures into categories: animals, things we eat	
Understands basic time concepts: tomorrow, this afternoon, yesterday	
Listens and follows a group story?	
Expressive language (speech and language output)	
Interacts verbally with a familiar adult	
Interacts verbally with other children	
Speaks using single words Speaks using phrases Speaks using sentences	
Responds appropriately to questions	
Relates a story/experiences sequencing events correctly	
Takes part in conversations	
Initiates conversations/asks questions	
Uses language structures appropriately: Pronouns Verb tenses Prepositions	
Uses non-verbal communication: Gesture/pointing Makes eye contact	

Comments:

Figure 6.6 Language assessment record

© Gill Thompson (2003) *Supporting Communication Disorders*, David Fulton Publishers.

7 Attention and listening skills

Attending and maintaining focus for concept formation, understanding, social communication and learning

Very young children will have a limited attention span and may be easily distracted. They are usually able to listen and focus if they are presented with something that interests them and can shut out other stimuli. If, however, a child is unable to control their own attention and is attracted by all the auditory and visual stimuli around them, they will find it very difficult to pay attention to verbal information in the form of a story or spoken instruction. They may not take in all of a verbal command or explanation, missing out words or phrases, misinterpreting certain sounds or failing to understand vocabulary. This will make it impossible for them to grasp the meaning and may leave the child thoroughly confused.

If you have completed a language assessment, you will already have some pointers to the exact difficulties that the child is experiencing. This should help you to identify which aspects of spoken language the child is struggling to understand. For example the difficulties may relate to:

- **Hearing** – the child may not be hearing certain sounds correctly, which will give a distorted version of the original spoken instruction. This may also occur if the child is unable to pronounce certain sounds, confusing one with another. This may lead to inaccurate perception of sounds.
- **Auditory memory** – the child may have a poor memory for the sounds of speech, words, short phrases or specific elements of verbal information, making it difficult to retain and process a complete sequence of verbal information. A sentence may contain too many units of information for the child to process. Continuous speech, made up of multiple sentences, can be impossible for the child to untangle, particularly if the pace is brisk. They may forget topic-related words quickly, needing a prompt card as a reminder.
- **Comprehension** – this relates to difficulties understanding the meaning of language concepts. The child may not understand the basics of colour, size, shape, position, time etc. or the subtleties of language as presented through pronouns, question words, negatives etc.

- **Processing time** – some children take longer than others to take in information, process it and respond appropriately. By the time they have done this, someone else has answered. They may just give up trying, as they never manage to get an answer ready in time.

We need to consider *listening* in two ways:

1. The ability to concentrate and pay attention
2. The ability to interpret and understand what is heard.

Both these components of listening are vital to allowing a child to access the curriculum and it is important to identify where a child is having problems and to provide support and intervention in those areas. Some children may appear to 'switch off' as if they do not see the need to listen, or they may become attracted to peripheral details, responding inappropriately. They may rely on watching what the other children do in order to carry out instructions. They may find it difficult to follow language that extends beyond the literal or requires them to interpret or infer.

Suggestions to help develop attention skills

Children who find it hard to concentrate in a group situation, when instructions are being given, will often benefit from simple devices to help them concentrate.

- A soft toy or ball to hold may prevent children from rocking on their chair or fiddling with other, more distracting objects. (I use juggling balls or 'stress balls' as they are tactile but not particularly interesting to look at.)
- Keeping language simple.
- Instructions may need to be broken down into simple steps – this can be done verbally or in the form of pictures/written stages which the child can refer to during the activity.
- Visual cues can help to reinforce the content or sequence of an instruction – pictures of the main components of the task can be stuck to the board as each part of the activity is explained (look, cut out, put in order, stick, write a sentence . . .).
- A teaching assistant or the teacher can then repeat these quietly, once the activity begins. Alternatively a laminated board with a 'velcro' strip can be used to sequence pictures that show the stages of an activity. They can be removed as the child completes each stage.
- A visual reminder to 'listen' (see Figure 7.1) can be placed on the board and pointed to if the child's attention wanders. (Reward good listening, e.g. using stickers on a chart.)
- The teaching assistant can be asked to watch for 'good listeners' and give a badge at the end of the group session.
- Ask the child to repeat all or part of the instruction – 'What have you got to do first? . . . next? . . . last of all?'

- Record instructions on Language Master cards (available from Drake Educational Associates, see Resources list) so the child can go quietly to hear the information repeated.
- The teaching assistant can introduce topic vocabulary prior to the lesson and a prompt sheet can be provided as reinforcement.
- Give time for the child to respond – other children may need to be reminded that it is not their turn to answer.
- Try to relate new instructions to the child's previous experience.

Listening games and activities

Listening skills can be taught through a variety of structured activities. These can be done with a group or individually. You will need to select or adapt the following activities according to the child's age and level of ability.

- 'Simon says' and similar listening games.
- Rhymes and songs with accompanying gestures – 'The wheels on the bus', 'Heads, shoulders, knees and toes' etc.
- Identifying animal sounds from a tape and matching them to pictures.
- Identifying sounds made by a variety of 'noise makers' which could be musical instruments, everyday objects (teaspoon in a cup, scrunched-up paper, beans in a jar etc.).
- Clapping a sequence.
- Joining in with a familiar rhyme, adding the missing word at the end of the line – 'Incy Wincy . . . Climbing up the . . . Down came the . . . And washed the spider . . .'
- Read a story containing the child's name. He/she must put up their hand/stand up every time the name is mentioned. This can be done one-to-one and then extended to a group using names of the other children. It can be made more complicated by asking all the boys to stand up if they hear a boy's name and all the girls when they hear a girl's name.
- Read a story and the child must select the appropriate picture as it is mentioned.
- Read a story and the child must play an appropriate sound effect as it is mentioned (thunder, raindrops, footsteps, bell ringing, animal sound etc.).
- Present a number of objects and ask the child to collect two or three items for your shopping bag (to feed a puppet, to take to school, to take on holiday etc.). Increase the number of items as the child progresses.
- Screen activities. These can be done one-to-one or in pairs, with one child giving the instructions. Use a screen to prevent the child seeing what you are doing and give instructions to be followed. This can be done with objects – 'Take the blue cube, put the red cube on top, then the green cube . . .' – or with pictures to be coloured or marked – 'Put a cross on the big house. Put a ring round the small car. Colour the small tree blue . . .'. If you carry out the same instructions as you give the child,

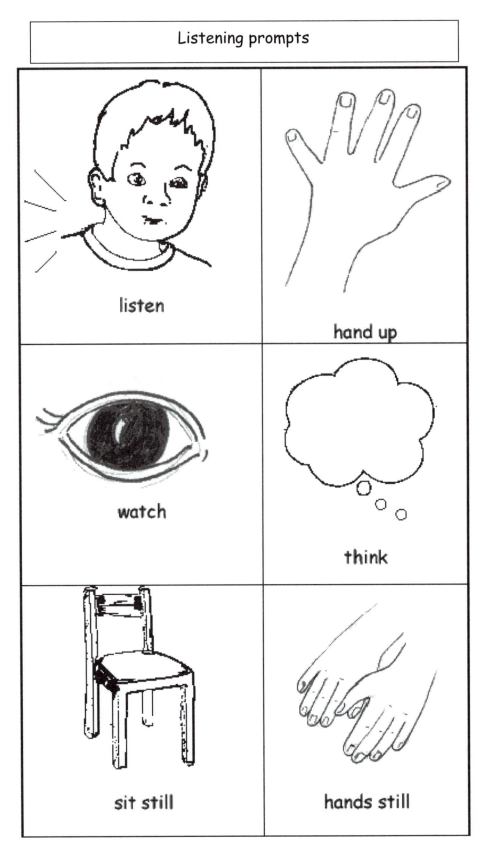

Figure 7.1 Listening prompts

you can then compare results and talk about them at the end of the activity. This activity can be adapted to all types of resources including felt shapes on a board, Lego pieces, coloured shapes, picture cards etc. – 'Put the man at the top. Put the car next to the tree. Put the cat on top of the house . . .'.

- Commercial listening activities can be very useful, particularly if the child can initially wear headphones to screen out any external stimuli and then later do the activities without the headphones.
- Number sequences – give the child a string of numbers that they can pick out from a set of 0–9 number cards. Start with three numbers and gradually increase to four or five.
- Pegboard sequences – give the child a set of coloured pegs and a pegboard. The child must listen to the whole instruction before carrying it out – 'Start with a blue peg, then two yellow pegs and then a red peg.' You may need to ask the child to repeat the instruction before doing it. Increase the level of difficulty as the child progresses.
- Simple sequences of actions – start with just two actions and then increase the sequence as the child progresses. For example 'stand up, touch the window', 'open the door, crawl under the table, sit down' etc.
- Give the child responsibility for taking messages – give simple one- or two-part instructions initially. Increase the number of things to remember as the child progresses.

The child needs to know that they are making progress and should have clear indication of success criteria. Don't expect too much too soon and be prepared to reward effort as well as success. Try to set short achievable tasks so that the child can experience success. I find that a sand-timer gives a good visual indicator of time passing and allows a child to work for up to five minutes before taking a break. This can be the limit to which a child is able to concentrate at any one time, but can be gradually extended once the child is able to understand what is being expected of him/her.

Social communication skills

Some children find it difficult to take part in group discussions, take turns, interact with other children and adults or respond appropriately because they are unable to comprehend the social rules that we all take for granted.

These children may be unsure how to join in with conversation, do not listen to others, speak out of turn and are unable to match their own speech style to the situation. It may be necessary to teach these children specific rules for different situations and give clear feedback when things go wrong. Instructions will need to be individualised and they will need to learn basic rules:

- putting up their hand if they want to speak or respond to a question;
- not shouting out if it is not their turn;
- listening when other group members are speaking;
- waiting to speak to an adult rather than interrupting.

They may need to learn playground rules and how to join in with play activities.

Circle time activities are an ideal opportunity for children to learn and practise simple rules, turn-taking, listening and joining in. Understanding that they can only talk when they are holding the toy that is passed around the circle; that they must listen so they know when to carry out an action; and that they need to look and listen as a clap or action is passed around are good strategies for encouraging the development of attention and listening skills, as well as social language and group participation. There are some excellent books by Jenny Mosley including *Quality Circle Time in the Primary Classroom* (Mosley 1996). There are also some good programmes available for teaching social language skills, for example Rinaldi's *Social Use of Language Programme* (2001) and materials for thinking through social situations, interpreting pictures and language. This type of programme is best planned in collaboration with the speech and language therapist who may be able to suggest some relevant activities for the individual.

8 Specific speech and language disorders

When a child has communication difficulties, it is usually the specific areas of difficulty that are immediately apparent and the impact that they are having upon learning. By analysing the child's speech and language, you can provide a basis for planning support and intervention in the school situation. It is also valuable to recognise some of the labels given to the various disorders, to understand the origin of the difficulties and the associated features that may be present. I have summarised some of the disorders that you may encounter in a mainstream classroom. (Further terminology is explained in the Glossary at the end of the book.)

Specific language impairment (developmental language delay, developmental language disorder)

Specific language impairment refers to all children with receptive and/or expressive language impairment without any associated features such as hearing impairment, mental or physical disorders. It may also be referred to as developmental language delay or developmental language disorder.

The areas of difficulty that come under this type of speech and language disorder can be in the following categories:

- difficulties with control of the speech mechanism – tongue, lips, jaw, breathing;
- difficulties producing the speech sounds and combining them to build words (phonology/articulation);
- difficulties using and/or understanding words, phrases, sentences (semantics);
- difficulties using and/or understanding the way that words are combined to form meaningful phrases and sentences (syntax);
- difficulties using language to convey meaning in a variety of contexts (pragmatics);
- use of intonation and stress in the production of speech.

A distinction needs to be made between language 'delay' and language 'disorder'.

- *Delayed* language follows a normal pattern and sequence of development but may not match the child's chronological age.
- A language *disorder* may present as a delay but it will become apparent that the development is not following a normal sequence.

Action

Use the assessments for language and articulation to provide a profile of the child's needs. Introduce activities for developing sound awareness, basic listening skills and improved coordination of tongue and lips (Chapter 4).

Work together with the speech and language therapist to plan a programme of intervention tailored to the child's individual needs.

Developmental dyspraxia

Dyspraxia is an immaturity of the brain resulting in messages not being properly transmitted to the body. It is a motor control disorder related to perceptual problems. Other names for dyspraxia include developmental coordination disorder (DCD), perceptuo-motor dysfunction, and motor learning difficulties. It used to be known as minimal brain dysfunction or clumsy child syndrome.

There may be associated difficulties with language, perception and organisation. Children with dyspraxia may have:

- gross motor coordination difficulties (PE lessons, running, skipping, team games);
- difficulty with handwriting, and drawing and copying skills are likely to be immature;
- limited concentration and listening skills;
- difficulty retaining multi-part instructions;
- difficulties as they may work very slowly and reluctantly in class;
- problems interacting socially with other children;
- difficulties sitting still for more than a short time;
- difficulties adapting to a structured school routine;
- difficulties as they may be easily upset.

Action

Children with dyspraxia can be helped by daily exercises to improve coordination and fine motor skills and may find that a writing slope, chunky pencil or wedge seat helps with maintaining a good sitting position for writing. (See the fine motor skills activities in Figure 8.1 and the Resource list at the back of this book.)

Hand exercises to help with the development of writing and fine motor coordination

(ensure that the child follows the exercises with his/her eyes)

1. Draw round the child's splayed hands on a piece of card or paper (this can be coloured by the child and laminated). Number the fingers from left to right (1–10).

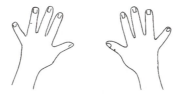

   The child should place both hands palms down on the table with fingers corresponding to the handprints. Touch one finger and the child should lift just that finger, leaving the rest 'stuck' to the table. Repeat for all fingers.
   See how quickly the child can match his/her own fingers to the hand pictures . . . practise.

2. The child puts both hands together as if praying. Ask him/her to bend in thumbs, then first, second, third and fourth fingers – straighten between each action.

3. The child should pick up small beads, grains of rice etc. and place them in a pot. Do this for one hand and give the child a ball or bean-bag to hold in the other hand. Swap over hands.

4. The child should pick up a marble or bead between thumb and each finger in turn.

5. Pincer grip: Using thumb and first finger, remove and replace pegs from a ruler – repeat with thumb and each finger in turn.

6. Hand flips: Place both hands on the table, palms down. Turn the left hand over. Now change hands, left hand turning palm down, right hand palm up. Start slowly and gradually increase speed and rhythm.

7. Star bursts: Place both hands on the table. Clench left fist, right hand outstretched – swap hands. Start slowly and build up speed and rhythm.

8. Hold a tennis ball in one hand and move each finger away from the ball, one at a time. Swap hands. Use a soft ball (foam or juggling ball) and squeeze/relax the fingers as they hold the ball.

9. Clapping games (work with adult or another child): clap hands together and then clap your partner's hands. Rhythm and sequence can be made more complex and the children can develop their own patterns.

10. Regular writing exercises: Roll'n write letters; draw letter shapes in a tray of sand; trace each finger around sandpaper letters before attempting to write the letter or trace over a shape on paper.

Figure 8.1 Fine motor skills activities

© Gill Thompson (2003) *Supporting Communication Disorders*, David Fulton Publishers.

Developmental verbal dyspraxia

Developmental verbal dyspraxia (DVD), (also known as developmental apraxia of speech and oral motor planning disorder) is a disorder affecting the child's ability to coordinate the speech organs for accurate production of speech. It is associated with developmental dyspraxia but the motor coordination difficulties may only be focused around the speech organs.

The symptoms of DVD are as follows, though not all symptoms will necessarily be present.

- The child may be late in developing babbling or may do little or no babbling.
- There may be feeding difficulties in infancy.
- The child may produce few consonants correctly and find it difficult to imitate tongue and lip movements or sounds in isolation.
- The child's understanding of language is usually much better than his/her expressive use of language.
- Speech production may require a great effort from the child and sounds may be difficult to distinguish.
- The child may experience difficulties in sequencing sounds to make a word.
- The child's attempts at continuous speech may be very hard to understand.
- The child may have problems controlling breathing and the speed, rhythm, volume and intonation for speech production.
- The child may make slow progress in therapy.

Action

DVD has an effect on voluntary speech movements. It is important to understand this aspect of the disorder and care should be taken not to put too much pressure on the child to communicate but to work indirectly on production of sounds. Plan a daily programme of general activities to increase coordination of tongue and lips and to develop sound awareness and listening skills. You may feel it appropriate to include some fine motor coordination activities (see Figure 8.1), as there are often associated features of developmental dyspraxia.

Seek the advice of the speech and language therapist for more specific intervention suggestions and for IEP targets.

Dysarthria

This is a condition affecting speech production, resulting in slurring of speech. It is neurological in origin and may be part of a developmental speech disorder or may be the result of acquired trauma to the brain as in an accident or neurological condition. The slurred speech is caused by a weakness in the movements of the speech organs. Where dysarthria is part of the range of symptoms related to cerebral palsy, there may also be impairment of receptive language and associated learning difficulties. There may be feeding difficulties and drooling.

Action

The speech and language therapist will advise you on how best to help and support the child with dysarthria.

Autistic spectrum disorders (ASD)

There are several groups of children who can be classified under this 'umbrella' term – children with Asperger's syndrome, semantic pragmatic disorder, pervasive developmental disorder, higher level language disorder (HLLD) and children with other variations of characteristics which fall within the criteria for autism. These children have problems with both verbal and non-verbal communication, finding it difficult to interact socially with others, to play imaginatively, to interpret language beyond the literal or to respond appropriately in a variety of situations. They may give poor eye contact and their body language may be unusual. There may be obsessive behaviours and inflexibility in responding to changes in routine. There is no conclusive cause for autism although it is now thought that it may be biological in origin.

Asperger's syndrome

Children with Asperger's syndrome have difficulty with the social use of language and need to be taught social skills and coping strategies for a variety of situations. Communication skills may be poor. Children may have an inability to express themselves appropriately via facial expression, gesture and body language. Their language skills may not match the situation and they may present as 'eccentric' in their behaviour. They are often obsessively interested in a subject, which they will become totally engrossed in, dwelling on it in conversation and attempting to draw others in to the theme. They can become socially isolated due to their poor communication skills and their 'different' behaviour.

Action

Teach a social communication skills programme (e.g. Rinaldi's (2001) *Social Use of Language Programme*), provide clear rules for specific situations and strategies for coping with social situations such as playground games and group activities. Discuss the meaning of texts, explaining how to interpret colloquial sayings, statements that have non-literal meanings, proverbs etc.

The speech and language therapist or educational psychologist may be able to provide ideas for a programme of support and intervention.

67

Semantic pragmatic disorder (SPD)

Children with this disorder have problems understanding the meaning of what other people say, and they do not understand how to use speech appropriately themselves.

Semantic means the *meaning* of words and phrases; **Pragmatic** means knowing *what* to say, *when* it should be said and *how* to say it. These children will usually have a good vocabulary, speak clearly and fluently but may also display some of the following features:

- delayed language development;
- learning to talk by memorising phrases, instead of putting words together freely;
- repeating phrases out of context, for example remembered extracts from television programmes;
- problems with understanding questions, particularly those involving 'how' and 'why';
- difficulty initiating, taking part in and following conversations;
- difficulty with non-literal use of language;
- difficulty taking turns;
- their level of understanding may not match their own expressive ability;
- difficulty with concepts such as 'feelings' or 'hierarchy'.

Action

Strategies suggested for Asperger's syndrome would be helpful with SPD. These children will need help interpreting facial expressions, discussing feelings and emotions, understanding what makes people feel happy, sad, angry etc. (see Chapter 4, Figure 4.3 'Facial expressions'). The rules of turn taking, conversation skills, question words, non-literal language will all need to be taught as part of a structured programme.

Down's syndrome

Down's syndrome is a genetic disorder, which usually presents with a range of difficulties associated with low muscle tone, learning difficulties and some other associated disorders (congenital heart conditions, hearing loss, chronic upper respiratory infections etc.). There are usually speech and language difficulties present but these will vary according to the severity of the disorder and the child's individual stage of development. For example:

- The tongue may have low muscle tone and appear large. Coordination of tongue movements is often slow and clumsy, which may affect the accurate production of speech sounds.
- The palate may be narrow and highly arched, making sounds made with the tongue and palate difficult – /s/, /sh/, /t/, /d/, /tch/, /j/, /l/, /r/.

- The Down's syndrome child may have frequent ear infections and 'glue ear', affecting hearing and auditory perception. The child may not hear sounds in the high frequency range or may not notice word endings.
- There may be difficulties with auditory processing – understanding and making sense of auditory information.
- Auditory memory may be poor.
- Receptive skills may be delayed.
- Expressive language skills may be immature and limited.
- Vocal quality can be hoarse and may lack intonation.

Action

Sign languages such as Makaton or Signalong (see Resources list) are often introduced to bridge the language gap and help with the development of speech and language. Early intervention with a programme of exercises to develop tongue and lip control and develop muscle tone is valuable. These children often have strong visual processing skills and these can be a useful teaching tool. Children with Down's syndrome need good role models for all aspects of learning and a well-structured programme to help them develop the skills needed to access the curriculum to their full potential.

The speech and language therapist will advise you on how best to help and support the child with Down's syndrome.

Fragile X syndrome

This is one of the most common inherited causes of learning disability. It is a genetic condition, which can be diagnosed by a chromosome test. There may be epilepsy present as part of this syndrome and children may have a larger head than normal. The child with fragile X syndrome may have concentration problems, be withdrawn and have poor social interaction skills. The range of learning difficulties may be mild to severe. Speech and language are almost always delayed and may display certain specific characteristics:

- perseveration – a tendency to repeat one theme or phrase as if 'stuck in a groove';
- echolalia – repetition of words or phrases said to them;
- articulation difficulties;
- low muscle tone may cause poor control of tongue and lips and may affect the soft palate, causing air to escape via the nose, thus affecting the quality of the sounds produced.

Action

Introduce general activities to increase awareness of sounds, tongue and lip co-ordination, and any specific articulation activities.

If speech and language difficulties are complex, seek the advice of the speech and language therapist.

Stammering, stuttering, non-fluency

Stammering, also known as stuttering, is the repetition of sounds, hesitations and silent blocks within words and phrases. Many children go through a phase of 'normal' non-fluency, when their expressive ability is unable to match the speed of their thought processes. It is best to allow the child time to express himself and to avoid pressuring the child to speak slowly or repeat the words. Listen to the child, focusing on the content rather than the fluency. Do not try to finish the child's sentence, and slow down your own speech so that the child has a good, clear model. This stage may quickly pass as the child becomes more proficient with speech. If, however, the non-fluency persists and has a marked effect on the child's ability to communicate, it is advisable to refer the child for speech and language therapy as the process of intervention is highly skilled and will vary from one individual to another. Children who stammer may feel embarrassed and frustrated. It can damage their view of themselves and make social and personal relationships difficult. However, it can be contained through speech and language therapy and the child can be taught strategies for coping with situations where they need to speak clearly. There may be associated 'tics' and breathing irregularities and the child may use avoidance techniques to omit words that begin with a specific sound.

Stammering can be increased when the child is placed under stress to speak aloud or when the child is excited, nervous or in a hurry. Be aware of situations that may be more difficult for the child, such as registration, answering questions in a group, expressing ideas etc. and try to give the child alternative ways of responding so that they are not placed in a situation that could trigger non-fluency in speech.

Action

The speech and language therapist will be able to advise you on how to support the child in the classroom and what targets to set.

Do not attempt to tackle this disorder without advice, as it can be made worse by drawing too much attention to the stammer or by placing additional pressure on the child. It is vital that the parents are involved in any programme of intervention and can reinforce any taught strategies at home.

Selective mutism

This condition is relatively rare and usually occurs in younger children. Some children do not speak in certain situations although they are able to talk freely at home or in more familiar settings. This condition used to be known as 'elective' mutism. If a child does not speak at school over a period of at least a term and their lack of communication is more than normal shyness or refusal to cooperate, they may be presenting with this disorder. It is a psychological problem concerning a state of severe anxiety and over-sensitivity.

Action

Refer the child to both speech and language therapy and educational psychology.

There may be underlying speech and language difficulties and the child will need to be assessed over a period of time with the cooperation of the parents. The child may talk at home and tape-recorded samples of speech may be used to analyse and assess communication skills. Make the child's school environment as relaxed and reassuring as possible and try to build a relationship based on trust and reassurance. Provide the child with opportunities to speak but do not place pressure on him/her to give a verbal response. Accept a whispered response or gestured communication and try to treat the child in the same way as the rest of the class as much as possible. Gentle encouragement to participate in group activities and non-verbal play may reduce the child's levels of anxiety.

There are other disorders that may have associated speech and language difficulties. You can find out about these from other publications or from the internet (see useful websites and addresses in the Resources list).

9 Planning intervention and support

Classroom strategies, suggestions for differentiation and IEP targets

Some children with severe speech and language impairment may be placed in a specialist language unit attached to a mainstream school but, with the current emphasis on inclusion and the frequent failure to identify communication difficulties prior to school entry, teachers increasingly need to be prepared to use a variety of different management strategies to teach and support the children in their classes. Communication skills are fundamental to the learning process and it is important that the teacher is fully aware of the child's individual difficulties and learning needs when planning the curriculum.

The classroom environment is important for all learners but may need to be considered in a new light to allow the child with a communication disorder optimum access to lessons. This may involve re-organising the way that activities are presented, re-thinking the classroom environment, providing access to additional resources and opportunities for appropriate, targeted support and for planning differentiated activities to support both learning and communication.

Assessment

- Work together with the SENCO to assess the child's skills;
- Determine the specific areas of difficulty;
- Determine the long-term objectives and specific short-term goals that you can aim to achieve with the child over a specific time-scale (six weeks, one term);
- Decide on strategies to be used and criteria for success;
- Decide on resources to be used (objects, picture cards, multisensory materials, speech book, school/home/clinic liaison book, Language Master, listening activities, worksheets etc.).

This information should be written into the IEP and incorporated into daily and medium-term planning.

Information

Get as much information and advice as possible from the other professionals involved with the child – speech and language therapist, audiologist (in the case of hearing impairment), educational psychologist, learning support tutor, occupational therapist, physiotherapist. Input from other professionals should be used to help with setting IEP targets and planning intervention.

Encourage a good relationship with the child's parents or carers, as they are a valuable source of information as well as being able to encourage and support the child at home. Even if they are unable to 'work' with the child, they can be helpful by being aware of the work you are doing at school.

Classroom management

The following areas will need to be considered for classroom management: hearing, receptive abilities, expressive abilities, associated difficulties and numeracy.

Hearing

The teacher will need access to information about the child's hearing ability and, if there is evidence of hearing impairment, how it affects the child. Where there is a communication difficulty it is important that the child has a thorough hearing assessment.

- Is there a constant loss of hearing or is there a fluctuating difficulty? This may be particularly relevant during the winter months when colds and ear infections are prevalent.
- Is the child able to hear better on one side or is there a need for the child to always face the teacher/speaker to enable lip-reading? This may affect where the child sits in the classroom.
- Does the child wear a hearing aid or need amplification? Special arrangements for this may need to be made and advice should be sought from the LEA advisor dealing with sensory impairment.

Ensure that everyone who has contact with the child – teaching staff, support staff, lunchtime and playtime supervisors, supply teachers etc. are all made aware of the child's needs.

Receptive abilities

Specific strategies may need to be used to encourage the child to listen, understand and follow instructions, participate as fully as possible in class activities and access special resources and support without drawing attention to the child or his/her difficulties. The child's understanding may be affected in one or more of the following ways:

- listening – level of ability to attend to instructions or information;
- concentration – limited attention span, easily distracted by visual or auditory stimuli, loss of focus if unable to understand;
- understanding key, information-carrying words but not the whole instruction;

- not understanding the language used by the teacher in verbal or written instructions;
- difficulties understanding basic language concepts;
- difficulties associating group instructions to self;
- not asking for help when it is needed due to anxiety, lack of expressive abilities or failure to realise when they have not understood;
- poor eye contact;
- sound location – the child may find it difficult to work out where a sound is coming from within the classroom and they may miss much of the content;
- difficulties focusing on the main idea, instead following a lateral or peripheral thought;
- difficulties with turn-taking;
- difficulties working cooperatively in a group.

Expressive abilities

The child's ability to use speech and language will impact on his/her learning, sharing of information with both adults and children and with forming social relationships. Poor expressive abilities may affect one or more of the following:

- intelligibility – articulation of speech, speed of utterance, fluency of utterance, tonal variation, breath control or volume;
- response to questions – there may be a delay in the child's ability to process and respond;
- sentence structure;
- sequencing skills;
- use of appropriate language in a variety of contexts – ability to assess the context, use of question/answer format, sharing information, conversation skills etc.;
- recounting experiences intelligibly – reporting back, recalling sequence of events, finding appropriate vocabulary and language.

Associated difficulties

The child with communication difficulties may also have related problems with reading, writing, perceptual and motor skills, which should also be considered. These may include:

- delay in acquiring sound/symbol correspondence;
- difficulties sequencing sounds for both oral and written tasks;
- difficulties with fine motor skills – pencil skills, manipulation of objects, puzzle pieces, self-help/dressing skills etc.;
- hand–eye coordination problems;
- visual perception difficulties – difficulties tracking from left to right, recognising letter/word shapes, finding detail in a 'busy' picture or diagram, copying from the board etc.;
- reading comprehension difficulties;

- self-organisation – difficulties finding belongings, remembering what to take to lessons, knowing what lessons they have each day and what books or kit they will need, homework etc.

Numeracy

Pupils with speech and language difficulties may have specific problems in numeracy, for example ordering and sequencing numbers, dealing with number vocabulary, comparisons, the relationship between spoken numbers and numerals, concept of odd and even numbers. An awareness of these difficulties can help with the way numeracy is presented and taught.

These difficulties may present themselves singly or in clusters and can make it very difficult for the child to feel confident as a class member and to learn effectively. There are, however, a variety of strategies, which can be used to provide a supportive classroom environment where these children can feel confident, secure and free to take part in the same learning experiences as their peers.

Strategies

1. Create a positive atmosphere in the classroom where mistakes can be made without fear of criticism or ridicule.
2. Consider seating the child where he/she can see and hear the teacher. If the blackboard/whiteboard is to be used, check that the child can see adequately without having to turn.
3. Encourage the child to look at you when you are talking.
4. When giving instructions, try to keep distraction and background noise to a minimum.
5. When possible, deliver instructions individually to the child, using the child's name. Some children may need you to actively gain their attention before they are able to attend.
6. Encourage the child to repeat instructions to determine whether they have understood (this could be done to a teaching assistant).
7. Do not 'correct' the child's speech but offer a correct model as part of your reply.
8. Teach vocabulary and topic words before starting a new area of work (this can be done by the teaching assistant or by parents). Teach about five new words at a time. (This can be achieved by over learning/ repetition, use of words in context, a word-bank with images as prompts and/or Language Master cards recorded with topic vocabulary.)
9. Allow the child time to process language before responding (other staff/ children need to be aware of this).
10. Rephrase, restate and simplify – questions and statements may need to be adapted so that they can be understood.
11. Instructions should be brief and appropriate (eight to ten words per sentence). Pause between sentences to allow for processing of language and for questions to be asked.

12. Use normal intonation and stress when you speak but do not speak too quickly.
13. In group discussions, repeat or re-phrase responses from other pupils.
14. Check for comprehension. Ask specific children to repeat the question or instruction.
15. Use visual cues, illustrations and props to reinforce understanding. This is particularly important when presenting a story, giving an introduction to a history, geography, science lesson etc.
16. When teaching reading skills, do not rely on a purely phonic approach. Use multisensory reinforcement (e.g. sandpaper letters, sand tray, pictograms, outline shapes around words, consonants in one colour, vowels in another etc.).
17. Give opportunities for the child to work in a quiet area to provide minimum distractions and to help with auditory foreground/background discrimination.
18. Allow short, timed tasks when attention is a problem (use a sand timer/stopwatch). Give breaks for the child to move around between periods of concentration.
19. Allow extra time for written work.
20. Accept a short piece of *quality* work rather than a longer piece of poor work.
21. Allow the teaching assistant to scribe for the child if the task is encouraging their ideas and creativity.
22. Use ICT to provide an alternative to writing – programs such as CLICKER 4 (available from Crick Software, see Resources list) offer a word/phrase bank, speech and pictures to encourage writing activities.
23. Use a Language Master to record instructions – the child can then hear the instructions repeated in easy steps.

When delivering the curriculum, remember the following:

S	Simple, short sentences – clear straightforward language
P	Pause between points or pieces of information
E	Enunciate clearly
E	Enthusiasm when communicating – use gestures and visual cues
CH	Check for comprehension

Individual Education Plans (IEPs)

Any child placed at School Action or School Action Plus level of the SEN register should have an IEP. 'The IEP is the structured planning documentation of differentiated steps and teaching requirements needed to help the student achieve identified targets' (DfES 2001a). An IEP should be a practical, working document that incorporates the main details of the child's learning needs, strategies for supporting the child and any specific intervention to be implemented, resources to be used and personnel involved. It should not be an unwieldy paper exercise that is kept in a file and never used practically.

Reviews should be carried out jointly between the SENCO and class teacher and, if possible, the teaching assistant so that progress can be evaluated and targets updated. IEP reviews should consider:

- the progress made by the child generally and in achieving targets;
- the views of the child and the parents;
- any new information or advice that is likely to influence the child's progress;
- the effectiveness of the strategies used to support the child.

Most schools review IEPs each term but, in some cases, the IEP targets may need to be amended more frequently if the child makes good progress. There are a variety of IEP formats used in schools and several commercial computer programs are available to make the process easier. The template illustrated here (Figure 9.1) is the one that I have found to work for me. It has been created as a template on the computer and information can be modified or added at each review. Parents are invited to contribute and they receive a copy of the termly IEP. Class teachers and teaching assistants have their own copies and 'review comments' are added by hand to inform the new IEP. Some children will have an IEP to address a range of learning difficulties and speech and language may be one part of the overall learning needs of the child.

Targets should be SMART (Specific, Measurable, Achievable, Relevant and Timed). It is unreasonable to set too many targets, as they are unlikely to be met. Include achievement criteria so that assessment of progress is specific. You may want to use the same resources as for the initial evaluation so that progress and achievement can be demonstrated on the 'Speech and Language Checklist' (Figure 3.6) or the 'Assessment of Speech Sounds' chart (Figure 3.4). Targets should be relevant to the child's needs and abilities and also to the work that will be done in class. They should be implemented either as part of the overall class activities or in one-to-one/small group sessions. These details should be indicated in the IEP.

Individual Education Plan

Name:	D.o.b.:
Class teacher:	Class/NC Year:
Date placed on SEN register:	
Stage: School Action/School Action Plus	
Date of IEP:	Review:

Assessments/involvement of professional agencies/referrals:
Ongoing informal assessment by class teacher/SENCO

Progress/achievements:

Areas of difficulty:

Receptive skills	Expressive skills	Following verbal instructions
Spelling	Reading comprehension	Social language
Sentence writing	Reading	Number skills
Listening	Concentration	Behaviour

Long-term aims:
Ability to access the curriculum at an appropriate level

Focus areas/targets:
1.

2.

3.

4.

Special educational needs provision:

Classroom strategies:

Resources:

Parents/carers need to:

Review – evaluation/outcome of targets:

Figure 9.1 Individual Education Plan

© Gill Thompson (2003) *Supporting Communication Disorders*, David Fulton Publishers.

Suggestions for speech and language targets

Indicate the time span for reviewing the achievement of targets, for example 'after six weeks' or 'by the end of term'. Suggestions for speech and language targets are:

- auditory discrimination – will correctly identify words beginning with target sounds;
- will imitate tongue and lip movements accurately;
- will use a straw to suck and blow;
- articulation – will use 'target' sound in initial/final/all positions;
- articulation – will use 'target' sound in initial blends;
- articulation – will use 'target' sound in continuous speech;
- will speak clearly when answering a simple question;
- will use 'I' rather than 'me' in spontaneous speech;
- will understand the concept of initial sounds and identify/recognise initial consonant sounds in c-v-c words;
- will answer a question or say his/her name confidently in a group;
- will use speech when playing with another child;
- will use speech to communicate with an adult (teacher, head teacher, dinner lady etc.);
- will carry out a two-part verbal instruction;
- will sequence events correctly when relating a personal experience;
- will correctly sequence four pictures to tell a simple story (assess with two different sets of pictures);
- will understand – on, in, under, behind, next to (assess with objects);
- will recognise colours – red, blue, green, yellow, black, white (assess with objects);
- will understand plurals (assess with picture cards);
- will speak with increased fluency (monitor number of hesitations in a set sample of speech);
- will speak audibly, with increased volume and clarity.

Conclusion

This chapter has brought together all the elements of the book – identifying speech and language problems, knowing when to make a referral for speech and language therapy, the developmental process of speech and language, assessment of both speech and language skills and ideas for activities to use with children once the difficulties have been identified. It has focused on the practical management strategies needed for successful inclusion of children with speech and language difficulties – addressing individual needs and including the child in every aspect of the school and facilitating access to the curriculum.

The process of inclusion is dependent on a whole-school ethos, understanding the diversity of learning needs and supporting the collaboration of teachers, support staff, parents and other professionals in delivering effective intervention.

Glossary

ADHD	Attention deficit hyperactivity disorder – characterised by inattention, hyperactivity and impulsive behaviour
Aphasia	a complete loss of speech and language skills (usually following neurological trauma such as stroke or accident)
Articulation	the movement of the articulators (larynx, tongue, teeth, lips, soft palate, jaws) to produce single speech sounds
Articulators	The specific parts of the vocal apparatus (larynx, tongue, teeth, lips, soft palate, jaws) that are used in the production of sound
Asperger's syndrome	an autistic spectrum disorder affecting social language skills
Auditory sequential memory	a disorder of memory giving rise to difficulties processing auditory information
Autistic spectrum disorders	a range of disorders which feature autistic characteristics (Asperger's syndrome, semantic pragmatic disorder, pervasive developmental disorder)
COP	Code of Practice (special educational needs) – part of the Government's education policy
CPS	County Psychological Service
Developmental language disorder	receptive and expressive language fails to follow the usual pattern of development (sometimes referred to as specific language impairment or developmental language delay)
DfEE	Department for Education and Employment
DfES	Department for Education and Skills (formerly DfEE)
Dysarthria	a neurological disorder affecting the movements of the articulators
Dyscalculia	a specific learning difficulty in mathematics
Dysfluency	stammer/stutter (also known as non-fluency)
Dysgraphia	a neurological disorder that involves the physical aspects of writing (e.g. awkward pencil grip or bad handwriting), spelling, or putting thoughts on paper
Dyslexia	a specific learning difficulty with reading, spelling and writing
Dysphasia	a speech and language disorder resulting from neurological damage – there may be a receptive loss and/or expressive loss. Developmental dysphasia is sometimes applied to children who have receptive and/or expressive language difficulties
Dyspraxia	an immaturity of brain function affecting the motor coordination system;
Echolalia	repetition of words or phrases said to the person

80

Expressive language	the production/output of spoken language
Final consonant	the last consonant of a word
Fluency	the joining together of sounds, syllables, words and phrases to speak smoothly and fluently without extraneous hesitations, blocks or repetition of sounds
IEP	Individual Education Plan
Initial consonant	the first consonant(s) of a word
Kinaesthetic	sensory feedback via touch and awareness of the body in space
Language	a rule-based system of communication which structures the sequencing of sounds and words for communication
Learning difficulties	'a significantly greater difficulty in learning than the majority of children of their age' (Education Act 1993)
Medial consonant	the consonant sound which appears in the middle of a word
MLD	Moderate learning difficulties
Non-fluency	a stammer or stutter – the repetition of sounds, hesitations and silent blocks within words and phrases
Perseveration	a tendency to repeat one theme or phrase as if 'stuck in a groove'
Phoneme	the smallest distinctive unit of a language which can signal a difference in meaning between words, e.g. /p/ and /b/ – pin/bin, hop/hob
Phonetics	the system of symbols used to write down spoken sounds
Phonology	the pronunciation of sounds in words
Pragmatics	the use of language in context, the development of purposeful communication, response to communication, participation in conversational interaction
Receptive language	the understanding and de-coding of spoken language
SALT	speech and language therapist
Semantics	the meaning of words and phrases in language
SENCO	special educational needs coordinator
Sensory integration	the combining of all sensory channels to learn and experience motor activities
SLD	Severe learning difficulties
Speech	the mechanical aspect of communication; the physical ability to produce sounds, words and phrases
SPD	Semantic pragmatic disorder. A disorder on the autistic spectrum featuring difficulties in understanding and using language, following instructions, reading situations
SpLD	Specific learning difficulties (dyslexia and related difficulties)
Stammering/stuttering	see non-fluency
Syllable	the unit of sound created within a word by the emphasis placed on it. A syllable is usually formed by a group of single sounds combining to form a unit of sound
Syntax	the rules used to structure language
TA	teaching assistant (also known as classroom assistant, learning support assistant, special support assistant)

References and further reading

Boehm, A. E. (1988) *Boehm Test of Basic Concepts*. Jovanovich, USA: Psychological Corporation/Harcourt Brace.

Cooke, J. and Williams, D. (1991) *Working with Children's Language*. Oxon: Winslow Press.

Daines, B., Fleming, P. and Miller, C. (1996) *Spotlight on Special Educational Needs: Speech and language difficulties*. Tamworth: NASEN Publications, in association with AFASIC.

Dennison, P. and Dennison, G. (1994) *Brain Gym (Teacher's Edition)*. Ventura, California, USA: Edu Kinesthetics.

DfEE (1997) *Excellence for All Children: Meeting special educational needs*. London: HMSO.

DfES (2001a) *SEN Toolkit*. London: DfES.

DfES (2001b) *Special Educational Needs Code of Practice*. Notts: DfES Publications.

Edwards, S. *et al.* (1997) *Reynell Developmental Language Scales III*. Windsor: NFER-Nelson.

Gesell, A. (1966) *The First Five Years of Life*. London: Methuen & Co.

Gray, C. (1996) *Social Stories*. Arlington, TX: Future Horizons Publications.

Hannaford, C. (1995) *Smart Moves*. Arlington, Virginia, USA: Great Ocean Pub.

HMSO (1993) Education Act. London: HMSO.

Lancaster, G. and Pope, L. (1989) *Working with Children's Phonology*. Oxon: Winslow Press.

Locke, A. and Beech, M. (1992) *Teaching Talking*. Windsor: NFER-Nelson.

Martin, D. and Miller, C. (1996) *Speech and Language Difficulties in the Classroom*. London: David Fulton.

Mortimer, H. (2002) *Special Needs in the Early Years: Speech and language difficulties*. Leamington Spa: Scholastic.

Mosley, J. (1996) *Quality Circle Time in the Primary Classroom*. Cambridge: LDA.

Portwood, M. (1999) *Developmental Dyspraxia*. London: David Fulton.

Rinaldi, W. (2001) *Social Use of Language Programme (SULP)*. Windsor: NFER-Nelson.

Ripley, K., Barrett, J. and Fleming, P. (2001) *Inclusion for Children with Speech and Language Impairments*. London: David Fulton.

Webster, A. and McConnell, C. (1987) *Children with Speech and Language Difficulties*. London: Cassell.

Resources, useful websites and addresses

Resources

AFASIC Checklists (speech and language screening tests) available from Learning Development Aids (LDA), Duke Street, Wisbech, Cambs PE13 2AE. Tel: 01945 463441. www.ldalearning.com

BPVS British Picture Vocabulary Scale (Dunn *et al.*) available from NFER-Nelson 414 Chiswick High Road, London W4 5TF.

CLICKER 4 available from Crick Software Ltd, 35 Charter Gate, Quarry Park Close, Moulton Park, Northampton NN3 6QB. www.cricksoft.com

Dunn, L., Dunn, L., Whetton, C. and Burley, J. (1997) *The British Vocabulary Scale*, 2nd edn. Windsor: NFER-Nelson.

Language Master Drake Educational Associates Ltd, http://www.language-master.-co.uk and can be purchased from various educational catalogues.

Learning Materials Ltd, Dixon Street, Wolverhampton WV2 2BX. Tel: 01902 454026.

Makaton available from Makaton Vocabulary Development Project MVDP, 31 Firwood Drive, Camberley, Surrey GU15 3QD. Tel: 01276 61390. Fax: 01276 681368. email: mvdp@makaton.org

'Sequential Thinking' cards available from LDA (see address below).

Signalong available from The Signalong Group, Communication and Language Centre, North Pondside Historic Dockyard, Chatham, Kent ME4 4TY. Tel: 01634 819915. Fax: 01634 814417. www.signalong.org.uk

Story sequences available from LDA (see address above).

'What's Wrong?' cards available from LDA (see address below).

Useful websites and addresses

Afasic – Association for All Speech Impaired Children. www.afasic.org.uk

Attwood, T. (1993) *Why Does Chris Do That?* London: The National Autistic Society.

Black Sheep Press – resources for speech and language support and intervention. www.blacksheeppress.co.uk

DfES website for SEN issues. www.dfes.gov.uk/sen

Family Village – a good on-line source of information on disabilities. www.familyvillage.wisc.edu/library.htm

I CAN – National educational charity for children with speech and language disorders. www.ican.org.uk

INCLUSION website – catalogue of resources for inclusion. www.inclusion.ngfl.gov.uk

LDA (Learning Development Aids) – suppliers of a wide range of resources including Language Master cards, listening activities, puppets. LDA, Duke Street, Wisbech, Cambs PE13 2AE. Tel: 01945 463441. www.ldalearning.com

NASEN, the National Association for Special Educational Needs – information and publications. www.nasen.org.uk

NFER-Nelson – educational publications and resources. www.nfer-nelson.co.uk

Royal College of Speech and Language Therapists – information and advice on speech and language therapy issues. www.rcslt.org

SEN The Journal for Special Education (Free magazine), Ribble Valley Publishing Ltd, The Wellfold, Clitheroe BB7 1LX. Tel: 01200 453000.

Senco-forum – valuable discussion forum on SEN topics. www.becta.org.uk or www.forum.ngfl.gov.uk

Special Children – The Questions Publishing Company, Leonard House, 321 Bradford Street, Digbeth, Birmingham B5 6ET. www.education-quest.com

Teaching assistants website – good information on specific disorders as well as resources and information on support. www.spare-chair.com

The National Autistic Society – books and leaflets, advice and support on autism and autistic spectrum disorders. www.nas.org.uk

Winslow Press – suppliers of books and resources for special educational needs. www.winslow-press.co.uk

Index